Etiquette

Most Common Etiquette Rules & Social Situations Where Etiquette Matters

(A Guide to Social Graces, Manners and Proper Behavior in Various Settings)

Charles Hicks

Published By **Zoe Lawson**

Charles Hicks

Etiquette: Most Common Etiquette Rules & Social Situations Where Etiquette Matters (A Guide to Social Graces, Manners and Proper Behavior in Various Settings)

ISBN   978-1-998927-49-4

Legal & Disclaimer

Table Of Contents

Chapter 1: What Is Etiquette

Etiquette actually manner manners. It way a first rate and settled precise protocol set up through civilization. It refers to the rules of behaviour. It governs our courting with others in our day-to- day sports. Social etiquette relates with our social relationship. Business etiquette specifically refers to the set of regulations governing the manner wherein professional human beings behavior themselves.

The phrase "etiquette" comes from a French phrase which means "rate price ticket." It at the beginning way the price tag that lets in someone's entrance inside the court docket docket ceremony in France. Some rules

were written at the charge ticket to make certain that human beings who have been invited to the feudal castle knew the way to behave together with the ceremony ought to run resultseasily. The idea of lifestyle is likewise rooted in our Vedic civilization.

Courtesy and ethical norms of behaviour are a part of our historic civil society. Respect, regard and correct thoughts-set are the marks of cultured and nicely-bred ladies and gents.

The substance of best manners is feeling and vanity of others. Accepted etiquette varies from u.S.A. To u.S. And from region to region. Good manners make us beneficial people of society. Importance of proper manners is stated below:

1.Good manners are vital for social in addition to commercial enterprise existence. One have to apprehend the way to behave; how to speak and the way to conduct oneself in society. Manners train you the ABC of cultivating a superb person and suitable social environment.

2.Good manners make you a fruitful member of society. They take you to the ladder of success.

3.Good manners assist you to live beforehand inside the aggressive business enterprise worldwide. One learns to stay in society. Getting a device or getting vending relies upon not most effective on technical functionality, however additionally on how efficiently you behave.

4.Your profession will go through, if you lack understanding of suitable business organization manners. Behaving like a expert helps you to live beforehand. Knowledge and workout of commercial organisation etiquette is critical for folks that aspire to obtain the top of their careers.

five.Good manners assist you advantage apprehend from others. As you offer, so you get. Hence, adopt right manners to end up an awesome social citizen.

6.Good manners produce worthwhile relationship with others. They

inspire cooperation. Manners act as lubricant for each day stresses while or more humans interact with each other carefully.

7.When you behave with apprehend and interest in the direction of others, probabilities are that they'll behave in the equal manner to you. Having proper manners can be of fantastic gain to you. In evaluation, lousy manners carry lack of buddies and clients. They tarnish your image and convey forth your lousy reputation. Good manners are first rate asset to extend the feeling of brotherhood, love and sincerity. So, usually undertake top manners and behave successfully and in such a way as your behaviour ought to be correct in each scenario.

Importance of Etiquette

Lack of etiquette is sure to ruin the surroundings in any business corporation. It may also breed considered one of a type enemies and unwell feelings. A guy who misbehaves with others showers insult on himself. Lack of etiquette makes one's person terrible. The guy can be handsome, well-dressed and good-looking in all respects, however his single act of misbehaviour can also purpose embarrassment to others and produce lousy impact to them. He can be having a awful or low social reputation.

So, one must constantly need to initiate others with correct manners and courtesy. The

mystery of turning into properly-mannered is simplest doing exercising and experience. You ought to be employer for adopting manners and etiquette of your ordinary existence for developing wholesome society.

The remedy for bad mannered humans is to deal strongly with them and turn them out from the company or avoid their organisation to deter in all sphere of life. There isn't always any doubt that one can not be a grasp of ideal behaviour in some unspecified time within the future of all sorts of situations. But you could despite the fact that maintain brand new proper behavior and unique grace all on my own.

There are women and men who brag an excessive amount of in any accumulating. Such people aren't preferred and left within the decrease again of in top society. While others, who do no longer brag about and deal in fact and respectfully with others, preserve normally improve in lifestyles.

The u.S.A.And downs in lifestyles come to all of us however well-mannered person can be capable of reduce them quick along together together with his presence of

mind. A character who considers the problems of others with cool head and enables them on the time of their misery is continuously reputable via way of others. A man or woman who's selfish is continuously disliked. One who by no means allows others can get no recognize in society. A individual with proper manners and etiquette may be a super guy. One who is confused receives irritated without hassle over trifles.

One's personality can expand properly quality if one has robust character and motion. A person is supposed to have accurate manners and etiquette best if he has a super ethical, will and character. It have to be continuously remembered that "Handsome is that good-looking does." It is a preamble for someone of particular manners.

Etiquette is not sincerely theoretical education. It must be tested and perfected almost. Only then you'll stay on pleasantly in society. It is a commonplace pronouncing that 1/2 of the war is already obtained in life, if one has proper etiquette and manners due to the truth with those tendencies one should face any scenario however

Chapter 2: Conversation

Conversation is an art of talking with others. While speakme we have to make sure that our speech is so audible that it want to be high-quality. And one should make sure that one's speech is not very loud as well. Good and proper communique is the primary issue of true manners. It is the place of speaking softly and lightly to provide a experience of most

courtesy established to the listener.

It is a primary reality of lifestyles that all of us craves for respect and if his self-recognize is boosted up, he can do a little difficulty with grace and

ease. There isn't always any doubt that there can be a relation between the giver and the taker. If the giver thinks that he has the right to command,   it'll harm exceptional's self-appreciate and he may be committing a blunder in his lifestyles. So, at the same time as speaking with loved ones, pals or every different character, the voice and way of speech need to in no way be hurting and must usually be soothing to others. The listener need to always feel that he's listening some difficulty educative, informative and well worth.

The conversation should usually be attractive with out being submissive; company without being offending and polite without being annoying. While speaking with others, one want to make certain that one ought to in no way talk from the mouth but one ought to do from the coronary heart and head. A cautious character ought to constantly weigh his phrases and talk satisfactory reasonable and applicable to the difficulty. Especially, while speaking with the ladies, one need to provide regards to them and never use harsh words or any form of abuse because of the reality the

ladies constantly have mild hearts and can't tolerate harsh and dirty phrases.

One have to also be more careful while talking with elderly person. The common rule is which you need to by no means harm one-of-a-type's emotions. It is a not unusual pronouncing that a wound because of a sword can be cured and dealt with however a wound due to the use of horrible phrases can not be cured and it hurts deeper in thoughts. So, you want to pay attention to all this on the time of communique.

First of all, you have to differentiate your communique as of public talking or non-public speakme. In public talking, one has to steering for formal verbal exchange. For this, one should speak with self notion. If the primary deal with is soothing and splendid, thousands of the purpose might be served.

Speaking is the number one element of conversation which have to be spoken softly and lightly to offer a enjoy of maximum civility. The way a person speaks is the principle

function to his achievement. Whatever you speak you have to communicate from the center of your coronary coronary coronary heart after weighing it. Someone has rightly stated— first weigh; then talk.

It is also actual that you want to not butter others and try to talk the truth. Sometimes fact may be painful but the manner you talk can reduce its ache. Thus, the position you have to have a look at in your speech is that hurting others is to be averted the least bit charges and you should commonly be a smooth speaker.

Polite Conversation

Some people are clever and carried out however shy. They discover one-of-a-type humans very difficult. Hence, it's miles profitable to discover how

to be assured and start super communique.

Body Language

You cannot keep away from speaking with others. Your body language suggests whether or not or no longer you are available. Like it or not, it communicates your emotions, attitudes and receptivity. A high-quality deal of body language which you display off is the cease result of conduct that you have unconsciously followed. Habits

can be changed with recognition and self-challenge. Identify them and consciously undertake the high-quality ones to beautify your image and receptivity to others. So, even as making communique you need to have smiling, an open posture, a leaning in advance, touching via a handshake, installing area eye contact and nodding on every occasion appropriate.

Posture

Having a superb posture offers stature and dignity for your photograph. This is vital in particular even as you're reputation or sitting inside the the front of a big target market or moving into a room complete of dignified dad and mom. Slouching offers a sloppy photograph. So, keep away from it.

Chapter 3: A Pleasant Self-Disclosure

You want to be cautious about appropriate and beside the point self-disclosure. Too plenty self-disclosure short might also have a poor effect. The stylish manual is to provide as an lousy lot statistics as you bought. Direction and timing are vital. Be observant. If you be aware a few element terrific about the alternative person, you could deliver a praise observed by using the usage of way of questions. You can create humour. Seek area of commonplace interest and experience.

It is crucial to listen. It is further critical to talk sufficient so one can

maintain a communication. Develop an area of knowledge that you find out exciting to talk about. Pick a topic in which your hobby is strong. Learn as plenty as you can. Develop your know-how in that location. This is one of the processes of growing your conceitedness.

Listeners need to be observant and aware of the verbal and visible clues despatched out thru others. You need to cultivate an thoughts-set of admire and elegance. To do that, it is critical to conquer the obstacles that save you you from listening powerfully.

If your mind is distracted with the aid of the use of manner of your very personal mind, you can't supply attention to what the speaker is announcing. Avoid interrupting. Avoid guessing what the speaker goes to mention. Remove all distractions out of your thoughts thru controlling your thoughts and emotions.

How to End the Conversation

It is essential to prevent the communique warmly just so every parties can also moreover sense extraordinary approximately the exchange that has taken region.

Interrupt at the first-rate juncture. Smile and prevent it up with an extremely good final sentence or a element thereof. Such as– "It is a pleasure speakme to you", "I choice for an early assembly", "It modified into top notch speaking to you", "But I want to go away now."

Be Sincere in What You Say

Be honest in what you are announcing. Use the other person's call. Maintain a pleasant open frame language; maintain eye contact; smile at and shake palms with the opportunity man or woman.

Avoid ending too or appearing impatient. The parting effect is as vital as the first have an impact on. Taking depart of a collection of people, you may make a mild bow and smile to everyone who takes place to be looking at you. Do not attempt to lure the attention of others who are not aware which you are leaving.

Ways of Improving your Conversation

When a 3rd person joins the communication, strive to draw him into the verbal exchange via the usage of briefing at the issue of communicate to the character. Accept honest compliments graciously with a "Thank you."

If a person asks you whether or not or not you want swimming, do not certainly say – "NO." This discourages communique. When in corporation of others, keep away from speaking about a private rely of which the zero.33 birthday party has no know-how. Ignore the presence of the people of awful manners.

Do now not spice your verbal exchange in reality to create drama and interest. Avoid boasting and bragging. Shun all horrible languages. Avoid asking questions which is probably too personal. Be cautious even as discussing topics in intercourse, coins and politics. Never ask people— "How a whole lot they earn or how masses did you pay for saree?" Don't correct unique people's pronunciation and grammar in public. Don't pinpoint weaknesses in front of others.

When speaking is in a fixed of three, try to have a have a look at the other people apparently so

that everyone feels covered. Do no longer touch the extra important man or woman to the exclusion of the primary character. Be cautious moreover in the manner you stand; supply enough region for the buddy to sense a part of the organisation. Learn to be comfortable with a touch silence.

In this manner, exercising to speak with a set with the aid of searching at all the suggestions and courtesy.

Meetings

Meeting is a system of making non-public contact with others in a civilized and improved way. In all the dealings with fellow human beings, one must present in an agreeable and presentable way to get the thoughts and desires via negotiation and persuasion as an opportunity of behaving rudely.

Meeting is the getting together of people of various capacities to talk about over a specific pre-deliberate state of affairs.

Business Meeting

Meetings are an crucial a part of enterprise lifestyles. The fee of meetings could be very excessive in terms of time. Time is coins in enterprise. So, assembly ought to be cautiously scheduled and deliberate. Your potential and manners are on display throughout the meeting.

Manners for participants at assembly are said below:

1.Dress well for enterprise corporation meeting. Do now not get dressed casually.

2.Come to the meeting a hint earlier. An govt must keep away from arriving later than the Person-in-Chair of the assembly.

three.When the ecosystem is informal, activities are unfastened to choose out their seats. When the environment is formal, junior executive need to make for senior ones to take their seats. As a famous rule, senior executives sit down at the rear of the

table and junior executives are seated similarly away.

four.If there are human beings already sitting inside the room, greet them. In a meeting outdoor the place of job, shake hands with all present beginning with the maximum senior. Introduce yourself to folks that don't recognize you.

five.Come prepared with relevant queries or elements to contribute. It is ideal idea to make notes. Avoid asking questions of less high-priced type.

6.Poor behaviour such as showing inattention, preserving private communique, or displaying signs and symptoms of the freedom or infection want to be avoided. Also keep away from violent warfare of words or emotional outbursts.

7.Be cautious of questions that could embarrass others. Avoid color jokes and flippant comments.

8.It is right to provide credit to a speaker who has made a valuable contribution or a massive detail.

nine.Do not taunt honestly everyone whilst you're in a assembly. Use proper and sober languages without hurting others.

10. After the assembly is concluded, thank the those who invited you to wait the meeting. Shake arms with those who have been present within the assembly and take go away.

Chapter 4: Greetings

Greeting is a system of revealing one's internal emotions inside the direction of numerous participants of

a family or society in dignified manner and well-tuned etiquette to create a congenial surroundings. Greetings are extended to unique people at specific activities. There are one-of-a-kind processes of greeting in incredible religions. We have to observe as in accordance.

By sending greetings to others one does no longer lose lots but gains lots more. Bitter relation becomes harmonious and on occasion antique foes turn out to be top and sincere pals.

One wins the coronary coronary heart of others in greeting each special. One sends one's splendid and honest feelings and suitable wishes that depend masses.

Smile and Laughing

Smile is a charming detail in the sphere of right manners. But smiles too often might also moreover represent insincerity of the individual. It is also genuine that exceptional conditions also can be resultseasily were given over with the assist of smiles. However, if a person is within the addiction of common smiling with out actual cause, the opposite detail might also moreover furthermore take offence secretly. A nicely-behaved man or woman have to be familiar with the paintings of proper intonation of laughter in splendid times.

Pretension

Smiles and laughter are one form of pretension but there are super modes too. A man or woman with a sugar lined tongue can be capable of hide his actual emotions and can make the opportunity character consider that he's taking a

authentic interest within the different's affairs. If someone is not irritated or does not display his displeasure in an open manner, he's showing accurate manners. A man of actual lifestyle and accurate manners does no longer fly proper right into a rage. It is also actual that pretended pride and suppressing one's anger can be without problems detected with the beneficial aid of a few other. Then, this pretention may additionally pop out as an evil of falsehood and dishonest.

In a civilized worldwide, a person want now not particular his innermost thoughts all of the time. Since an quantity of cowl is also vital.

Natural conduct is maximum mind-blowing. If someone has to maintain correcting etiquette, he have to behave manifestly and typically within the brilliant possible manners without artificiality. It is said that from time to time a 'NO' is extra full-size than an all of the times 'YES.' A man has to installation himself further to help others in the restrict of his functionality. He has to make his mark within the worldwide. He has to be socially useful as well. If he inns to faux, his friends won't recollect him dependable and in the long run he can be within the loss.

Telephone Courtesy

Conversation way to talk with others to alternate views. A acceptable communication also can be made on cellphone. In a face to face verbal exchange you're capable of see and understand via facial expressions and unique forms of frame language. You get on the spot comments as to whether your message is thought. In a telephonic verbal exchange you're not capable of smile to indicate which you are best and receptive. You want to use immoderate great words or phrases to talk a awesome thoughts-set and tell others that their call is valued and welcomed.

You need to cultivate a pleasing voice. A super voice is one that shows no indication of annoyance, indifferences, infection or over pleasure.

Treat every name as an opportunity to bring together super dating. It creates proper will and establishes appropriate report. And an extremely good record is installation through welcoming feedback and displaying your problem for the caller.

Incoming Calls

A famous rule is that the telephone should be picked up inner three rings. Being it converted from one department to each other is likewise a reasonably commonplace experience. That is the advice to all personal vicinity employers to well educate and equip their employees with the applicable facts to cope with the customers.

Taking Notes

There ought to constantly be a pen and notepad inside rear to take down any important be conscious or message from a cellphone call. It isn't appropriate to keep the caller waiting for longer time. Writing message is useful to bring in its actual revel in. So, make a addiction of making

vital message with the decision of caller and calling time. If the decision is bureaucratic, file this in a file for future use.

It is always higher to use high terrific terms and phrases on cellphone. It is the artificial for smiles and facial reputation. Never use terrible terms proper now. Try to make your language notable by way of the usage of the usage of the phrases like "OK, I can, or I'll try my stage wonderful" in area of pronouncing "I can't."

Have a remarkable finishing with courteous language at the same time as you finish your call .

How to Introduce

Being added to one-of-a-kind and introducing others appear frequently in lifestyles. When you're introduced to others, don't forget the following:

Rise

It is suitable for each- girls and gentlemen to upward thrust as a mark of apprehend to famend an introduction to a woman or different guy. In social conditions, your obligation is to benefit understand of a social reputation.

Facial Expression

We can not neglect about to emphasise the advantage of a grin. It makes you appear friendlier, warmer and additional approachable. A first-rate and first-rate facial display will growth your man or woman. So generally smile. It is a nice non-verbal signal. A smile suggests preferred approval closer to the opportunity man or woman. This will make special man or woman feel more receptive and friendly closer to you.

Chapter 5: How To Introduce Others

Sometimes you get a chance to introduce others. The extra junior person is delivered to the more senior and important person.

A female is brought to a gentleman. When each are of the same intercourse, the young man or woman is added to the older one. Members of a circle of relatives are delivered to those outdoor the family.

Title is normally not used in introduction except the man or woman added is as an alternative incredible or masses older.

A new employee should be introduced to his instant manager. Proper creation should be made to human beings with whom new employees will come into contact within the course in their artwork.

Self-Introduction

There may be activities while it's far essential to introduce your self. If you enjoy uncomfortable, steering to conquer your nervousness or awkwardness. Your self-introduction need to make human beings recognize who you're. It offers stimulation to begin your conversation. Your self-advent

need to be right and enthusiastic. It need to be high-quality. If you've got been delivered to someone who seems to have forgotten your call, do now not be afraid to re-introduce yourself.

Manners are the simple factors to civic existence. So, one ought to have a look at them to manual efficiently in a single's existence. Manners have their magic. As quick as you magnetize them, your person draws properly proper fortune.

Fine Feelings and Symbols

For getting to know suitable manners, one want to have a few capabilities to undertake them. One need to have the feelings and symbols for first-rate manners. You additionally have some mind of behaviour predicted of you. They are supposed to be outward symbols of 1's appropriate emotions and attention for others.

See the Positive

To strike it rich, you want to pass deep and soak your character in accurate mind for

others. To accomplish that, see the excellent elements in their merits and achievements.

Feel Good approximately Yourself

Be happy with the state of affairs you are in and the quantities you've got. In distinctive terms revel in accurate approximately your self. Be grateful to God for all of the advantages He has bestowed upon you. To be thrilled with yourself is the route in your going up the ladders of fulfillment.

Think of Other People

It is an difficulty of not unusual information that folks that consider different's element of view are clever human beings. Those who consider others make substantial efforts. They are extra green; more beneficial.

The subject of your body need to boom to the manner you figure, stand, take a seat down, preserve your chin, and so on. Your faces want to be active and mirror electricity. In no way need to the have an impact on take transport of of dragging the toes and rubbing the ground. Each step must be company and high quality

of path whilst not having anxiety in mind or strain on thoughts. Standing, too, ought to mirror energy. You want to stand upright with out a stoop. Your legs ought to show firmness, not stiffness.

While sitting, cultivate the dependancy of preserving your decrease lower back erect except you're a laugh. You appearance clever that manner. And your thoughts is more active as well. You want to open an air of recognition and success. The chin have to be fairly up. Don't permit it to drop because it indicates defects, gloom or self-obsession.

Grooming

Besides you need to appearance appealing, you need to ensure that your hair, clothes and footwear are in order. All your garments need to be properly-washed and nicely-pressed. Your footwear want to be polished and hair pretty reduce and combed. Don't swing to the intense of gaudiness. You can effects distinguish amongst smooth,

respectable, properly-pressed garments and pretentious and gaud ones.

Spoken Behaviour

Decency need to increase to all of the factors of without a doubt everyone's behaviour. It is brilliant to be natural and sincere. It is indecent to be pretentious and showy. The second any character pretends, it's miles unnatural.

Gesture

Every individual is endowed with a exquisite persona. His speaking, recognition and all wonderful actions need to be in tune with this individual. It is one of the foremost guidelines of etiquette that one need to look at or have a look at not to the touch and circulate one's goods. A man or woman should now not in fashionable contact every other person's frame besides he is probably very near. When someone is talking to some other individual, it is not an splendid manner for him to move his fingers or enhance his shoulders or toss his head now and again.

Repetition

Repetition might be very stressful to the person who has to be aware about all this. If a person repeats, it would imply that the person distinguishing the matter is doubtful. However, a one-of-a-kind situation may also additionally additionally rise up whilst repetition becomes vital. If the listener is familiar with subjects wrongly, the paintings and mind may moreover get spoiled and losses also can incur. Then, repetition of the contents is essential.

General Behaviour

There are a few factors of elegant behaviour which we would really like to speak about as under—

1.You need to placed the topics lower again on the identical vicinity from in which you have were given eliminated. It is a point not handiest of courtesy but additionally of highbrow comfort.

2.You must be punctual. Being past due offers the photo of being no longer dependable. It erodes humans's self belief in us; the most precious commodity in this worldwide.

3.You want to honour your phrases in your very own interest. If out of place, your credibility may be at stake and it'll deliver you down in humans's estimation.

The factors referred to above are virtually guidelines on each day mannerism. They are not all specific and complete. They aren't exhaustive alternatively illustrative. The need is to increase properly revel in and attention for others.

Entertainment

Entertainmentisapartofetiquette. Without information of etiquette you may in reality't entertain site visitors well. There can be methods of exciting. Lunch-on is a mid-

day occasion.

It is also a quick affair of entertainment. Home entertainment enables to customize corporation courting. It is extended to them who have end up friends. In a few corporations, it has emerge as a traditional annual affair for employees. It is terrific to entertain business organization buddies. On the sports, every time you

are invited to the residence of your boss, colleague or organization companion for a completely unique lunch, you should follow a few recommendations like this:

1.If you are conscious that just a few pals are invited, do now not speak approximately the affair to the ones not invited to keep away from sadness or misconception.

2.When buddies or employees are invited to a home for lunch or dinner, it is normal to encompass spouses. The companion should meet the possibility visitors. It might be useful to provide some ancient past information approximately the host. This will assist in beginning an notable communication and asking sufficient questions all about.

three.It is asked as a well mannered gesture to convey a small gift. The present have to in form the recipient, no longer the giver. Avoid costly objects which may additionally additionally recommend bribery or motive embarrassment. Check your company's insurance received as gift.

4.It is regular for the hosts to greet their commercial enterprise friends or employees and then introduce their spouses to occasions concerned.

5.Suitable sincere compliments at the right second approximately the house layout or décor need to take delivery of.

6.Conversation on the tables have to include own family people and spouses.

7.Do now not request to go to the interior a part of the house, if no longer favored via manner of the visitor. You want to no longer peep apparently into the bedroom. However, ought to the host invite you to see the rest of the residence, be organized to definitely take delivery of gracefully.

eight.Male site visitors need to do not forget to wear linen socks without holes in. Take off your shoes even as moving into the room.

nine.The huge rule isn't always to live for a couple of hour after dessert and espresso. Remember to thank the host for the hospitality at the equal time as departing.

10. If using the bathroom, go away it in easy kingdom as you noticed it while you first entered.

Friendly

The lunch can be organized at specific tiers. One must address the location and age. The older the age of the lunch birthday party participants, the calmer can be the tone of amusement. Attending to an man or woman lunch birthday celebration, it's miles a famous rule of etiquette that one must now not tease or criticize or be scornful in a unmarried's behaviour to 1's buddy in such a celebration.

It is probably horrific manners to reduce quick speaker earlier than he has completed genuinely because of the fact time is over. It is permissible to lessen jokes, if the celebration takes vicinity to be amongst friends. Young human beings need to now not take a seat so close to with matured or elderly people.

It is essential for the traveller to meet the host and the hostess on the earliest possibility. Meet the host and the hostess on arrival and on the time of departure. It is also regular for anyone to co- characteristic the host or hostess and to render some assist or be geared up to carry out that.

Always try now not to be past due as it is thoughtless to hold others ready. If the host is late and expresses to be difficult up, he need to telephone the eating place and characteristic someone bypass a message of apology in addition to statistics approximately the expected time of arrival. Instruction that the visitors be attended and cared for must also take shipping of to the perfect character. Late for extra than ten mins need to be apologized.

Sitting

The host must see that every one the visitors are seated in advance than he or she sits down. Unfold your napkins and lay it in the route of your lap. Whenever critical within the course of ingesting, use it to moderate contact and smooth your mouth. Do no longer wipe vigorously. When leaving the desk, location it loosely to the left of your plate. Don't fold or depart it on your chair.

Posture

Sit in an upright characteristic on the facet of your elbows off the table. Do no longer slouch. Ask the waiter for recommendation in advance than making your choice and setting your order.

It is the obligation of the host to ask his visitors if there may be any meals they want to keep away from for the cause of fitness, religion, medicine or alike. The tourist's orders are usually taken first; the host's orders ultimate. Beware moreover of the diploma of familiarity triumphing on the eating place.

Don't spend too much time on thinking over what to reserve. It does no longer supply a splendid have an effect on. Don't order for food this is too hard to grapple with. It is appropriate to begin talking over business or profession as soon due to the fact the orders for foods and drinks had been positioned.

Be powerful to sum up your statistics at the surrender of a dialogue to ensure that there can be a meeting of minds on what we mentioned.

Paying the Bill

When honestly all of us has completed the meal, ask for the bill. When it's far brought, you may take a look at discreetly and rapid to confirm its accuracy. If it's far accurate, pay off right away. If there may be discrepancy, you could take a look at with politeness. If you have got a few special versions, excuse yourself and settle at cash desk.

Chapter 6: Family Etiquette

Charity starts offevolved at home. It is an vintage announcing. It shows that one has to research to expose consideration to individuals of one's own family. Father, mom, brother, sister, servant or even the pets have their very very own area inside the family. The proper etiquette that may be careworn in the family is to behave in a

manner.

Father

Father is the pinnacle of the family. He has the maximum responsibility. Chanakya, the famend Indian statesman and economist

of historical instances, said that "As the pinnacle of the circle of relatives is, so will the particular individuals of the family be." Father won't be aware of it but each member of the family underneath him is asking the subsequent step that he's taking or approximately to take. If the daddy trains his people of own family nicely, his little youngsters can also regard him for all time.

Father has to set the guidelines of etiquette within the residence and has himself to test them actually and completely. He has to educate the youngsters to greet one another pleasantly. He has to train the kids to be respectful toward their dad and mom. Child is a tiny, touchy soul. It is like easy clay which can be moulded whichever way its mother and father desire.

If a father behaves extra or a whole lot less collectively collectively with his kids at each new come across, their ego may moreover get harm and it's far possible that they will growth quite a few awful behavior when they develop up. In this line of principle, it'd be incorrect to reserve one's children about and deal with them in the identical manner as servants or

subordinates. Hence, father has to stand at the helm of affairs on all conditions. He has to persuade the own family clean of waters by means of manner of his very very own strategies.

Mother

"Give me appropriate moms and I will supply you unique country" –Napoleon is stated to have remarked as quickly as. Without mom's benevolent artistry, no own family can develop nicely in this strife-ridden global. The sweetness and heat of a mom permeates into the coronary heart of all the individuals of the own family. Father may be the formal head of the circle of relatives, but it's far the mom who brings up the family and trains the more youthful. Just as a toddler learns to articulate in the mother's language, so as does it studies from its mother the crucial etiquette in life. There isn't always any crime extra heinous than to neglect approximately this contribution of a mom in a unmarried's life. It is the mom who teaches the child a manner to behave with others. If by manner of threat, the mother, because of lack of expertise or otherwise, transmits her wrath or feeling or revenge to the child, it can growth as a whole lot as be a depressing character afterwards. The little one has no way. It learns some element it's miles taught. It is handiest the mom's watchful eye that may discover wherein and on the same time as the child is going incorrect.

She appears after the small statistics of personal cleanliness, protection of highbrow and bodily fitness, strategies of sitting, standing and talking in a first rate way. Her rebukes are loving. A mom must be business enterprise with a misbehaving little one, but motherly love and encouragement counts most. The mischief completed in the easy years of childhood won't be taken too critically besides terrible behavior begin forming within the toddler in a deep-rooted manner. Nor is the coverage of taking the whole lot to daddy to be applauded. A mom who complains often or is simply too strict may additionally additionally herself be instrumental in dropping her maintain on her children.

The domestic need to be an area for co-operation, not war. And the harmony among mother and father is vital for the implementation of any rule or principle.

Children

It is within the right upbringing and development of kids that the beliefs of a own family are fulfilled. Children want to get preserve of their first lesson of etiquette in the family. It is probably wrong for the mother and father to depart all the responsibility to the academic organisation in the upbringing in their children. Even if the child is placed within the pleasant business corporation, the dad and mom or guardians want to preserve an eye constant and notice that the kid won't take a flip in lifestyles for the more serious.

In the house itself, the toddler learns a way to behave with numerous family and friends. A infant want to discover ways to address elders in a respectful way. A precocious and demonstrative child can be

interesting to look at however whilst the limits of civility and orderliness are passed, a infant may additionally moreover end up a stressful detail to an intruder and embarrassing to its dad and mom. The fault might not lie with the child itself however with those who are supposed to be in charge of it. A misbehaving infant should straight away be taken to task, whether or not or no longer or now not in public or in a personal location. A incorrect as soon as overlooked has a tendency to multiply. But whilst it is checked at its first occurrence, it may disappear all the time.

The toddler might also pose all its instincts and inclination in the uncooked. It can also devote or can be vulnerable to dedicate one mistake after another. If the guardians lose want effortlessly and brand the kid as mischievous or incorrigible, it's miles the child who could be lost certainly. It is well to remember that a infant is vulnerable to correction while much as the adolescence age. Gentle phrases, politeness, hassle, obedience, enjoy of obligation, private cleanliness, and so forth. Are to examine to a toddler in

its early and impressionable years. This is the duty of mother and father and dad or mum.

The baby should not touch extraordinary's matters. It should not intervene and skip reviews when elders are speakme. It must keep its mouth close while chewing meals. It must not accumulate dirty conduct like sucking finger or putting it in nostrils, etc. It have to not be present within the corporation of elders longer than critical. It must apprehend its feature within the own family and in any business enterprise. It want to moreover have a look at to say its prayers regularly. It ought to gain knowledge of to attend its turn at desk and no longer clutch meals out of flip. It need to expose recognize to the alternative intercourse. A toddler who becomes a bully is coward at heart and is loser in any competition.

These information of every day dealing and the manners of normal residing are not to be made routinely. Strictness need to furthermore have its limit. Admonitions and rebukes are to be aptly punctuated thru love, faith and mutual consider.

Servants

It can be wrong for a servant to brood over his venture or employment within the family and endure in mind himself a dejected and solid-off man or woman. A servant has an vital element to meet in own family existence. If the mother and father are professional or place of work-goers or in any other case preoccupied, it's miles the servant who can also look up the youngsters in decide's behalf.

Chapter 7: General Etiquette

Proper right here are a few etiquette and manners in society through which the pattern of life of

Someone from his early life is decided. There is some etiquette to be displayed specifically on the equal time as attending activities, ceremonies, video games and sports activities via shaking hands with, embracing or wishing every exceptional in befitting manners. One ought to analyze from others a manner to maintain one's bearing and dignity in all activities. When you speak of large etiquette you need to understand the way to provide yourself with correct manners continually in high-quality situations consisting of at college and

college, in sports sports activities floor, throughout ceremonies and activities, at home or out of doors, in mattress-room, drawing-room, and lots of others. You need to recognize the manner to address ladies, gents, kids, pals and elders.

Colour of someone is uncovered while you take a look at him at the equal time as he is quarrelling with others. During such state of affairs one need to have strength of mind. One has to workout this super inside the initial diploma of life. If one lacks in self-schooling and self-control, you may't keep one's particular manners and etiquette even in a pleasant environment. Real manners in ordinary occasions will show one's inherent culture. A properly-cultured guy is privy to all of the paraphernalia of etiquette below specific conditions, collectively with welcoming, great and bidding farewell to friends and individuals of the family. He speaks with considered considered one of a type tones to his spouse and youngsters, friends and superiors. He is also first-rate in speakme to his juniors or inferiors. He typically encourages his juniors to talk frankly and in fact with him. His

techniques of sitting, fame or doing some thing will always be decided with the resource of his juniors or seniors. His traits will provoke others and will persuade that he's a person with correct etiquette and manners.

Business Manners

Businessmannersarethosemanners which without a doubt absolutely everyone carrying organization have to analyze, undertake, schooling and inculcate in him to make his business organisation a first-rate fulfillment. The primary purpose of a businessman need to be his contribution to the society. Nobody expects a businessman to promote his gadgets at a loss. On the other to this ethics, he want to additionally not cheat the general public. There ought to be company ethics. Making of earnings want to be inside the framework and mind of business employer. Otherwise an act of such commercial enterprise corporation may additionally degenerate right proper right into a criminal motion. Nobody

would like a businessman to have massive income at the fee of his clients.

A sensible and smart businessman generally attempts to inspire his guys to artwork freely however surely. He isn't always required to disturb them unnecessarily of their job. A wonderful form of possession mind-set is a downside to the improvement of commercial enterprise business enterprise. Something is to be built up with the help of employees and customers. A proper businessman should forget the photograph of 1 man show. One can extract most gain from one's personnel, if right dignity is tested to them.

If he has to flourish in his commercial agency, he has to have right courting amongst himself and his humans. He must in no manner lose his mood and rebuke his humans within the presence of others. If any corrective action is needed to be taken in the direction of any of his employees, it's miles constantly better if it is taken in personal and never in advance than others.

For any outsider traveling for any scenario, the number one effect is the remaining have an effect on.

This paramount impact is created with the resource of the reception office. Whenever an interloper visits any place of work, he need to right away be attended and asked to sit without difficulty, and immediately moves want to be taken to satisfy the desires of an intruder.

The behaviour of the personnel of reception place of job specially is predicated upon on the strict instructions as to a way to deal with the honor, reputation and performance of the concerned in the public eyes. The behaviour of the employees located at decrease level of any problem is the replica of the place, strictness, kindness and manipulate of the owner towards his employees. If the owner is selfish, rude, short-tempered and inefficient, the personnel walking below him might also tend to act within the same undesirable manners.

The leader or owner of any employer should now not supply a incorrect notion in his thoughts that he's the main pillar in his company over which the complete of it is based upon. It is he who has to make regulations and comply with them strictly and

complete-heartedly. The boss who sermonizes but does not act on his non-public is on occasion taken in a severe way or obeyed willingly. The place of organization may be located into threat, if the boss does not inspire proper behaviour and supply proper treatment to others. The boss need to never rebuke or scold a supervisor before his subordinates otherwise the general performance in desired will go through.

In fact, an enterprise may be helped by means of way of the small interest and authentic conduct with special related humans. Everybody within the project need to installed his efforts to carry suitable. It is the customers and terrific acts that carry nicely name, popularity and profits.

In any business enterprise business corporation sincerely every person is counted. All have their operating inside the employer trouble to meet their obligation well worth of their position. All need to offer assist. All should should do the artwork fast. It is, therefore, important that every man or woman should greet each other in a pleasing way. It is a horrible

way, if an employee talks sick about his employer company. Always preserve it in thoughts.

Customers' Part

Every customer is an honourable individual for any businessman. Good family individuals amongst vendor and customer may be set up best with the useful resource of mature information. The businessman who is concerned in bargaining and canvassing over prices has now not something to do alongside with his non-public insinuation. It is regular for any businessman to revert once more to regular situation after bargaining. To show as an terrific businessman one should watch and test lawyers- how they do the arguments with every one-of-a-kind and greet each other after being attentive to of the case. So, it should circulate within the identical manner in each sphere of existence. Business is likewise one of the video video games being finished the various provider and the customer. It additionally ought to be achieved within the spirit of a real sportsman. The businessman need to hold his personal feeling and negotiation spirit one by one. He

ought to not enjoy damage, if the bargaining and canvassing is as an alternative hard for him.

Chapter 8: Etiquette Related To Hospitality

Entertaining a Guest

S regular with the Indian mythology a GUEST is constantly considered as an incarnation of

God and is normally reliable and handled as such. But in reality, a visitor is a visitor handiest until he behaves properly and stays for a few days with the host. A character is a group in his personal residence and will become a vacationer in different's residence on the equal time as invited on a particular occasion.

The visitor need to take shipping of proper mattress tea, breakfast, lunch and dinner on time. His all comforts, however little or insignificant may be, are to be furnished to him with a smiling face. The more youthful inside the family have to reveal appreciate to him and all antique people of the circle of relatives need to bathe love and blessing at the visitor.

The visitor should in no manner be allowed to experience uninvited or unwanted. The tourist on his very very own aspect has to in form his propensities to the region of the host's residence and need to attempt to keep away from any embarrassment of through any way type it could be to his host. The traveller need to usually try to regulate himself inside the host's house in the sort of manner as he may not feel himself a burden by way of the use of way of the host. The traveller can be greater eager on reading novels, magazines, books or staying indoor than taking element in outdoor sports. He can also require more privacy for his relaxation or comfort. His meals conduct may be unique than the ones

of host with whom he is staying. Certain sort of food may not be genuinely to his liking. In such activities the visitor has to modify himself with anybody and the whole lot in the house of the host. The traveller need to forget his troubles and try and keep away from exposing his anxiety. He must continuously present himself in his most captivating and snug face.

The host family people need to be virtually skilled in the art work of looking after the goals and comforts of the traveler as a long way as possible. This is a part of correct etiquette inside the direction of the visitor. All the contributors of the host family want to make sure that monotony or dullness does no longer attempting to find in progressively into their behavior with the visitor. Equally vital it's miles for the traveler to ensure that he does no longer stay any in addition. The 2d he realizes that he isn't any more welcomed as a visitor, he must make a few excuse and leave for his very very own residence and say good-bye to the family people of the host. In turn, the family individuals of the host ought to show not unusual

courtesy with the beneficial aid of extending suitable recognize and regards to the departing traveller.

There are a few factors which should be taken in account via using each- a vacationer in addition to a set. Though host's obligation is high-quality, the traveler should no longer forget about the etiquette of a first-rate visitor. Host need to examine those elements:

Duties of the Host

1.He have to be well prepared for welcoming the guest.

2.He want to make proper affiliation for tea, meals, lunch, and so forth. He want to not try to make display off with highly-priced gadgets.

three.He must show love and admire for all site visitors similarly.

four.If the visitor comes inside the starting time, he himself must be in satisfactory way.

5.He need to make the guest sense snug all of the time. He has to keenly be aware of all of the dreams and necessities that a traveller needs.

6.He need to comply with all of the manners and etiquette to be placed on the identical time as attending him.

7.He ought to now not permit the tourist revel in bore. So, he must talk with jolly mood and provide exclusive assets of enjoyment like magazine, newspaper, TV, and so forth.

8.He need to deliver a heat goodbye on the surrender of the entertainment.

Duties for the Guest

1.He need to now not go to to the host without informing him. It is higher to provide a call in advance.

2.He need to continuously supply a few shape of present, which may be culmination, sweets, and so forth. For the host or his family.

three.He want to take care of the timing which have to now not be weird.

four.A traveler want to usually combo with all.

5.He want to now not make show of his wealth with the aid of boasting.

6.He have to now not overeat or drink past his functionality. In contrary, a few website site visitors sense shy and not take a few issue. It is a bad addiction which ought to be averted.

7.He should be superb and agreeable. He need to depart his problems and troubles inside the again of at domestic. If he sits with reminding of his sorrows, he's going to no longer be capable of behave properly. He must not be at host's residence for longer period.

8.He should thank for the meal praising the fun meeting. He can also offer a praise to the host.

Chapter 9: Etiquette Within The Institution

Head of the Institution

nstitutions are of extremely good importance for building up the character and profession of

a scholar. The Head of institution is the path finder for his institution. He won't have direct contact with college college students all the time. But his hobby and issue for the students is continuously ahead of all.

It is crucial for the foremost to make every day rounds to look that the whole thing is so as and the rules formulated are discovered with the aid of using all.

To make this supervision more effective, it is probably recommended for the Principal now not to maintain to a regular schedule but to be out within the university corridors at unusual periods without any be conscious. This may additionally additionally maintain all of us on his toes and the examine- up of the policies may additionally hold with out trouble. Miscreants and mischief-mongers in the college need to be punished and their agonies and embarrassments need to be made exemplary. But there should be equitable treatment for all. The Principal is shape of a father of the institution and, consequently, he has inner his fold, no longer excellent college college students but teachers and others related to the faculty. Nobody can or need to question the authority and superiority of the Principal. But he need to have sympathy and recognize for extraordinary teachers.

It may be taken into consideration a terrible manner to remonstrate or take a trainer to project in public or inside the presence of college students, because of the reality such motion can also moreover moreover demoralize the lecturers and make the students undisciplined. In this example the errant teacher need to be recommended in my opinion about his fault. He need to usually assume for the betterment of institution, teachers and university students.

Teacher

A teacher in real experience tries to behave flawlessly. The non-public man or woman and disposition of a teacher are proper for college college students who could not handiest want to comply together with his coaching but additionally his instance in nearly all subjects.

Teaching is a top notch responsibility which want to be fulfilled cautiously. The teacher who has been capable of keep aside the two factors of his persona- his normal self and his training self may be at peace with himself. It is probably beside the point for a trainer to take advantage of his superior feature and employ his students to serve his personal pastimes.

A teacher who misbehaves and abuses college students inside the lecture room or out of doors won't be granted to be in his role. It may be a

mistake on the a part of a instructor to fight with every different instructor in the presence of college college students or to decorate the letter in his non-public affair. There may be situations even as university college students revel in for their teachers and want to realize greater about their private existence and so on. At this time it'd be cheap to open coronary heart for them. But the keynote is love and expertise of college students. There want to be some guiding elements in a teacher's career.

Student

Students are the beginners. They want to get a few element of schooling which may be taught. Students need to be within the apprehend of the diagnosed codes of well-known behaviour. They should be well informed approximately the rules and hints. Art of learning from the instructor is generally seemed to the wise and crucial pupil.

Students need to expand a experience of devotion, reason and self-apprehend to their instructor. They need to treat their college as a temple of know-how. In the identical

way, recognize for instructors is need to for all university university students.

Employees and Workers

The personnel and the personnel connected to establishments are to differentiate themselves from their colleagues in precise repute quo. Institution personnel must domesticate a completely particular kind of zeal and devotion for his or her paintings. Responsibility of younger ladies and men hired in an organization cannot be belittled. They need to simply accept apprehend and addressed as Sir or Madam.

All these ladies and men need to train themselves to build up the vital dignity just so beginning from the Gatekeeper to the Office Superintendent — all ought to regard the institution as their very own and ought to artwork loyally to decorate the quantity of the students in their company and take delight in such improvement. This mentality is extra critical in nurseries and number one schools.

No count what the some time of the scholars in the company can be. Everybody in the college ought to artwork for strictly keeping the location of the business enterprise. The wrongdoers must be because it need to be said for his or her misdoing and need to be punished. A excellent obligation rests on the Gatekeeper of the organization who has been instructed not to permit everyone out in a few unspecified time within the future of school hours.

The administrative center workforce may be entrusted with the motion of critical circulars about examinations, checks, tutorials, opinions, expenses, tours and so on. All of which may additionally have a exceptional bearing on the lives of college students. Institutional artwork requires a super sacrifice, social spirit and co-operation with out which the development of the scholars may be significantly retarded.

Parents

Teachers and parents every assist masses for the development of youngsters. Without co-operation of dad and mom, instructors can do

not some thing. By co-operation of the each, a baby is capable of having a everyday improvement. If a determine gets his toddler admitted right right into a splendid organization and shuts his eyes clearly to its development, there are opportunities that the child won't gather the preferred famous of success. To make it a truth, the mother and father must be in detail concerned inside the typical performance and behavior of the kid.

The determine-trainer courting need to be based totally on a supplementary and complementary mission. There should be sympathy, mutual assist, fellow-feeling and right information. It is for the mother and father to recognize the paintings and burden of the instructor and co-carry out him in every way. His shortcoming, if any, may be introduced to his knowledge and he also can have the opportunity for retracing his step or changing his approach of teaching.

On his element, the trainer has to preserve in thoughts that the father or the father or mother may additionally additionally

produce other duties or he may have a large own family. If there is right and properly timed co-operation a few of the teacher and the mother and father, they will meet at together convenient hours and remedy matters thru discussions. To set up this kind of dating, it's far expedient for the dad and mom in addition to for the lecturers no longer to lower each one in every of a type within the scholar's eyes. The determine must building up at domestic the sensation that the trainer can do no incorrect.

Chapter 10: Other Etiquette And Manners
Sitting

Ne must pay hobby whilst he's sitting, especially to his posture. In first rate situations, for instance — in lecture room, in institution, as a vacationer, the posture can be one in every of a type.

While relaxing, you may sincerely take any posture. For extraordinary situations, cope with a few factors. While performing for an interview for a project, one need to discover ways to sit properly. Positioning and motion of hand at the same time as showing some shape of gesture mark the first-rate of one's

man or woman and nature. Tremor in a single's hand, however insignificant it is able to be, shows a diploma of anxiety and anxiety in a single's thoughts. While sitting at the chair where table is there in the front, one have to location one's palms properly each on the handles of the chair, on his lap or on the desk in front. The function of legs is likewise very crucial.

While sitting at the chair contrary to individual interviewing, one want to in no manner shake one's legs beneath the desk and make sure that legs want to now not be extended in this sort of way as it starts offevolved offevolved hitting or touching the leg of an interviewer. These are taken into consideration to be very terrible manners. Sitting nicely want to be frequently practised even in normal day-to- day existence with the spirit of the wonderful stop result.

The art of sitting isn't always an result in itself. One need to be cautious that his have an effect on is marked at the same time as he starts offevolved offevolved talking. While speakme, one want to now not exchange one's posture of sitting and feature to talk in a polite manner, specifically,

pleasantly and concentrated on one speak inside the form of way as awesome's interest is not diverted.

Standing

The excellent function to be followed even as status is that one need to stand immediately with palms every facets on or locked at the back and ft a touch apart.

While coming close to an interviewer, typically bow a bit to show recognize to him. Standing with hands on waist or biting nails or popularity on one leg, putting more weight on one leg and bending to the edges little is the worst shape of status. It proves that the man or woman attending interview lacks proper manners. Such postures reputedly display disrespect to others. Hence, such attitudes need to not be exposed on formal events.

While attending or looking after VIP, one must be typically attentive to the selection of the VIP and should now not screen a informal attitude or laziness inside the path of the VIP.

While talking to another person, you need to pay entire hobby to. This presents a quite picture for others to test. It additionally appears greater remarkable to others. When one is a bunch at a rite and is responsible for welcoming the guests on the same time, he need to appearance within the direction of all elements and be aware of the desires of others supplying a healthful and smiling face. The guests have to experience relaxed within the route of the birthday celebration.

As far as feasible, the host within the path of birthday party need to make himself comfortable in recognition function at some point of the function and must now not supply have an effect on of self-vanity.

Speaking

A man or woman with unique etiquette and manners have to recognize initially how to speak in a correct manner. The most important part of speech is the shape of get dressed which should constantly be soothing and first-rate. If this is long-established as a dependancy, 1/2 of of the warfare is constantly received in first hand itself. Speaking is also an artwork. The manner someone speaks can cross an prolonged way in bringing fulfillment to him. Some of the human beings experience that their boastful approach in speaking can also moreover furthermore supply them achievement in existence and it can be one of the exceptional approaches of impressing others. But this isn't always accurate in any respect. It is a very not unusual saying that you are paid within the identical cash, i.E. If you are polite to others in speaking, others will even routinely be polite to you. One can extract most artwork advantage from one's subordinates thru cajoling, pampering and high-quality behaviour and particularly alongside together with his way of speaking to them with sweet phrases.

You must normally be candy and actual for your speech, for the reason that artificiality may be determined out very without troubles. One should study the paintings of speaking in any other case as required for every awesome scenario.

Whether you're talking collectively together with your pals, household or the possibility, your voice and way of speech need to be soothing

and appealing. One want to be company in a single's speech with out being offending, and polite with out being worrying. One need to not speak beside the point phrases and must now not blast out a few component comes on one's tongue. One must weigh the terms before speaking. Only less expensive and relevant phrases should come out from one's mouth. One need to continuously communicate the truth now not denying the fact. Avoid something that is painful.

Games

Your lifestyles is grew to emerge as out to be a few kind of a venture and you're gamers in it. You want to fight and score both for the crew you're playing or for self however the maximum crucial purpose must stay playing in sportsman spirit. Game have to be finished for the sake of pastime. You have to play with the best of efforts and have to play really with out dishonest all of us.

A individual who is scared of going thru the rival pretty as consistent with the tips of the game may also find out it tough in lifestyles to face the battle. In the

initial degree of lifestyles, a baby need to advantage knowledge of the art of combating his warfare himself and consequently, he can research his lesson tremendous in the gambling subject or in any recreation.

The injustice lessen on the part of player or referee ought to not be tolerated and need to usually be damaging. If you are within the right, even the spectators and others searching the game will provide you with complete guide on your honest and sincere efforts. You should study the orders of your captain. Always document for the sport to your proper pastime gears and in time inside the subject and co-carry out in conjunction with your institution-pals. It bureaucracy an exceptional dependancy of sportsman spirit and inculcates problem among sportsmen that is the number one detail in the sport and may be very vital for the group. Always keep in mind that one team simplest has to win and the other has to lose the game.

Chapter 11: Psychology Of Personal Marketing

The fact that worldwide has modified masses in modern-day years does no longer endorse that actual manners and the recommendations of etiquette have fallen into disuse. On the opposite, the ones guidelines are even though greater alive than ever, and they are although capable of constructing a noticeably outstanding personal photo, mainly within the commercial employer worldwide.

They are vital for executives who need to launch in private advertising and marketing. That's why in advance than we communicate about etiquette and appropriate manners, it's miles suitable to understand how the psychology of private marketing works.

There is a herbal property of the human mind that expenses us with an purpose for all of the things we apprehend. Since it's far almost no longer feasible to have an purpose behind all topics, we usually generally tend to return once more to phrases with wonderful "standards" that society admits to be actual. These are called "conventions".

Here's an example: no character is going to Mass or an vital rite wearing swimsuits, is it? Xinguem acts like this because of the reality there can be a convention that establishes guidelines regarding clothing appropriate to remarkable conditions. It is those conventions that make up the size of valuesof human beings, groups, and societies.

"Convention is all this is traditional - with the useful resource of the usage of trendy consent - as a norm to maintain and to behave in social existence."

When you behave in line with the dimensions of values   of a particular organization, it's miles

preferred by using that organization. However, while you do not act or smash a convention, you are situation to interpretations which can be past your control. You may be seen as a person of "a few exceptional corporation" and right now away from it.

"All symbols - shades, shapes, behaviors, and so on. Patterns - are related, mentally, the default pics and people pictures, almost constantly, are formed from 'social conventions' private environment we stay.."

It is well to remember that each person is seen regular with our non-public judgment of right and wrong, in step with our private trouble of view and our very personal pastimes. Only others see us from exceptional angles, from one-of-a-kind angles, and, no longer once in a while, see records that we do not even recognize.

Therefore, the tremendous thriller to real personal marketing and advertising and advertising and marketing is to project your photograph thru already agreed symbols and which may be feature of every social business business enterprise.

That's why cultivating correct manners, cautiously following the social protocol, is the high-quality mystery to having a sturdy and green advertising and marketing.

Some styles of immediately highbrow institutions:

Symbol Convention

Book Culture, intelligence

Suit Status

White Peace, cleanliness

Smile Good schooling, generosity

Tie Respect, reputation

Gold Refinement, expensive

Good manners Status, refinement

Jewelry Luxury, arrogance

Sticker

How we're "evaluated"

The end stop result of the whole thing we do is predicated upon on how we relate to important human beings, how we introduce ourselves and the way they interpret us. This is also authentic even as it comes to looking for a interest or negotiating. After all, we do no longer exchange with machines, however with excellent human beings.

People have a look at us in each the technical and the behavioral factors. The voice intonation, the posture, the manner to sit down down down, to eat, to greet, the whole lot displays the individual, everything is evaluated.

So, a smooth handshake or perhaps the way to have a coffee, can say masses about you. All of that is an imperative a part of a seen / behavioral set that passes statistics on who you are, who you are.

Chapter 12: The Glasses Gafes

at meetings and commercial enterprise lunches are very common, even some of the most professional executives.

The word "gaffe" comes from the French Gaffeur, who is not something extra than the person who commits gaffe. There are 3 sorts of people who devote gaffes: folks that assume, individuals who cowl, and those who try to remedy.

Contrary to what many human beings count on, one need to no longer try to recuperation a gaffe. Gafe dedicated, assumed gaffe. Because, while looking to repair, the tendency is to make the situation even worse.

They typically appear for lack of common sense or due to the reality the person values topics that the alternative does no longer value, or due to the reality they despise a few element that the extremely good values too much. That is why we verify that prudence and common enjoy are infallible guns to keep away from gaffes.

"If you're making a mistake, it is extraordinary to allow it pass, because of the truth worse is attempting to healing it." Etiquette

Chapter 13: Rules To Comply And Present People

Etiquette hints are a form of code thru which we inform others that we're   prepared to stay harmoniously in the employer.

These policies basically address social conduct, beginning from the manner to get dressed because it need to be to the various events, to the tactics of ingesting, to attending public areas and, chiefly, how to narrate to human beings. So permit's start thru speakme approximately greetings and displays.

There is a easy rule for all kinds of presentation: every body who's appearing or being delivered need to smile and look the character in the eye. Seriousness and tension do not paintings nicely in shows.

Another rule says:

"The most vital individual is who receives the alternative and has his name said first. In the enterprise surroundings, it's far thrilling to provide the consumer this extra significance."

But if at the time you have got got doubts the high-quality is:

Present the person to the female.

Present the youngest person to the oldest.

Present a colleague to the consumer.

Present any person to the traveller of honor.

Follow the ones protocol commands:

1 - When you are proven, if you are seated, the person must rise up. This rule applies to men.

2 - If you do not stand up, it may seem which you are disinterested or unrelated. 3 - Women, if they're seated, should simplest upward thrust up if the man or woman supplied is the hostess or an vintage lady.

4 - When it's as a whole lot as you to introduce a person, say the man or woman's

entire name and some difficulty to start a verbal exchange.

5 - The "howdy" and the "how's it going?" are considered elegant compliments. You do no longer should use that conventional "masses pride!"

6 - The ladies also shake arms.

7 - If the lady is attending a gala occasion, she does no longer need to take off her gloves to greet. However, keep in mind to take them out in case you consume.

Another essential trouble that need to be determined - each thru the usage of women and men - is that the pat at the back and the kisses should continuously be averted, except there may be outstanding intimacy amongst them and the occasion lets in this form of affection.

It may moreover rise up that the person provided - for the sake of discourtesy - does not acquire out for compliance. What to do? If with the useful aid of stretching your hand to introduce yourself to someone, she does not reciprocate this gesture, withdraw your hand however hold the presentation. This mind-set is accurate.

To introduce someone to a group, experience the instantaneous you are together and say a few element like this: "Hi, men, I preferred to introduce you to Luciana Forli, Briattore designer in Milan."

Also apprehend that handshakes are distributed in group shows.

An vital recommendation:

When you introduce yourself to a person, do now not name your self doctor, trainer, and so forth.

Chapter 14: The Handshake

The handshake is a shape of compliance that want to obey a few regulations of etiquette, for the reason that it is capable to mention lots approximately a person.

The label says that the more youthful individual does now not attain out until the older individual does, certainly as someone have to not gain out to a woman each. But if a person reaches out to us in a situation that is in violation of some rule of compliments, it should not be refused. A law that should be respectable with the useful resource of all says that no prolonged hand can stay inside the air.

- To avoid gaffes, and as customs range from society to society, the maximum reachable is a brief success, without an excessive amount of pressure and without truculent movements.

"But no matter a easy handshake we must be cautious. This is due to the fact, in Asia and the Middle East, you do now not shake arms while you greet someone, as this is interpreted as an competitive gesture.

- In Islamic international locations, engaging in out to a lady is quite offensive.

- In Japan, as in different Asian countries, bowing in advance than some different character, is a bow that corresponds to a handshake, with the particularity that the person of decrease popularity curves earlier than and under.

- Thais and greater traditional Hindus also do not shake hands. They positioned their arms together on their breasts and bow earlier than every exceptional.

You who excursion, want to pay close to interest to the ones info.

Note additionally:

Common enjoy recommends that we have to commonly be privy to high exceptional particularities popular of companies or even international places. For example:

- Calling someone with the useful resource of stretching the curved indicator is, in lots of locations, offensive. For us Brazilians, it's far, at the least, rude.

- The OK signal made with the index finger and thumb collectively, which in Brazil is an obscene sign, in maximum countries is virtually herbal.

- In Bulgaria, people shake their heads backward and forward to say sure, as opposed to not.

- Touching human beings with their arms is not advocated if you are inside the United States. Already inside the Arab international, keeping a person's hand - or even going hand in hand - is proof of friendship and respect.

But there are different data concerning the posture that have to be observed, see:

- Standing with at once back and chin up is the very photograph of self-self belief and ambition.

"Hands within the returned of you-at a time on the equal time as you do now not understand what to do with them - is   an mind-set that also passes the idea of beauty and authority. Besides, it is so masses

higher than stuffing them on your pocket.

Crossing your fingers over your chest may moreover provide you with a protecting or battle of words picture.

- During a communication, an incredible signal which you are worried and paying interest to what you listen, is to lean barely beforehand and react to what the alternative says with a moderate nod or a discreet smile.

Chapter 15: Acting With Prudence

Experienced executives regularly avoid gaffes only excelling in top taste for the correct education, no longer making remarks of a non-public nature, specially even as you do no longer understand the individual they may be travelling or negotiating.

Therefore, to have an outstanding presence in a meeting or interview, the perfect is to collect as a exceptional deal records about the character you are going to speak to. Then, based totally on this statistics, you could select what is exciting, handy, pertinent.

There are severa strategies to get this information:

1 - Let's believe you're searching out a manner. If it is a consulting of desire of experts, it is important to apprehend how is that this consultancy, how it works, and masses of others. 2 - If the approach interview is inside the agency that you are hiring, then it's miles right to have the maximum records approximately this

organisation, the individuals who paintings on it, and so forth. This may be executed via the consultancy itself this is deciding on the applicants, or of individuals who recognise the enterprise organization.

3 - Entering the enterprise business enterprise's internet site moreover works, at least to apprehend what products it sells, what its philosophy is, its vicinity ofknow-how.

One need to no longer leave to hazard the chemistry that we commonly anticipate to acquire in an interview or negotiation.

15

ETIQUETTE RULES AND MANNERS I

Chapter 16: Thanking The Interview

For an government, it's far proper to continuously thank him for the opportunities which might be given to him. Especially, of path, thanks for the opportunity to had been interviewed for a venture.

This is a normally unnoticed step, however one which can be decisive for buying the process finished. By doing so, you will be displaying yourself to be moderate and polite, and also will preserve your call sparkling in the interviewer's memory. Do the subsequent:

 1 - Send the letter within the future after the interview.

2 - Check the selection and emerge as aware of of the interviewer, and make sure which you wrote efficaciously. You can also even request the cardboard because of this, or check with the secretary or the business enterprise agency receptionist.

three - Be formal in remedy, using "lord" or "woman". You ought to first-rate surrender the formality when you have a preceding courting, or if the interview has been comfortable and a success. In such cases, too much formality also can sound fake.

four - In the text, thank the interviewer for the danger given to you to reveal your professional traits. Describe some virtues of the interview, along with an interesting alternate of thoughts and an super possibility.

5 - Make it clean which you are very inquisitive about the vacancy and open to one of a kind possibilities.

6 - Add a few terms that display your hobby. For instance: 'I turn out to be pleased to peer employee delight in the business enterprise,' or 'Sales figures are amazing.'

7 - Describe your expectations. An instance is to mention that it'll include the visionary spirit of the organisation president.

eight - Finalize your letter with the same old closures, such as 'regards,' 'truely' or 'grateful'.

nine - Check spelling and print on authentic tremendous paper.

THE BUSINESS CARDS

At paintings, the label recommends the use of business agency gambling cards. It is a expert, stylish posture that may make appropriate contacts.

Cards ought to be small, smaller than a credit score rating card, discreet, however should offer numerous contact options, together with mobile phone, mailing cope with, email cope with and private website address, if any.

You can also use a short adress kind card (self-adhesive that consists of your address and contact huge range). These are extra practical due to the truth they can be pasted at once into the character's time table.

Never give up your card at the start of the communication. They need to handiest be brought at the end of a communication, or, in advance than it, to the secretary of the individual with whom you will have a assembly.

17

Your voice need to sound calm and excellent, but this is overworked. And take into account: the caller must draw close up first.

This rule must remarkable be damaged at the same time as the alternative extends the communication too lots and does not understand that it's time to reveal it off even when you say you're too busy or have an urgent appointment at that time.

One well mannered manner out is to break the verbal exchange by means of the usage of the usage of saying "It have become wonderful to acquire your name, but I want to hold up." If it although does now not turn off earlier than, you could flip it off first.

LABELING WITH THE ELECTRONIC SECRETARY
Scraps

and recording messages need to be quick. It is inconvenient to record a long soundtrack, or leave funny messages.

Likewise, whilst being spoke back via an answering gadget, messages want to be brief. Record your name, date and time you known as, a contact telephone amount, and, if important, a precis of the undertaking being dealt with. Here's an example:

Recorded message:

"Hi, I'm Rodrigo Padova and that is a recording.

How to transport away the message:

"Dr. Rodrigo, this is Otacilio Câmara, from GrafiSul. I need to talk approximately the Seminary in Brasilia.

Label For man

A black or army healthful, white shirt, undeniable or striped silk tie - with out extravagant prints - and properly-polished social footwear is a traditional ensemble that fits for each occasion.

In a primary assembly, particularly, the tie is important, despite the fact that no one in the organisation makes use of it. It can be a sign of respect for that surroundings.

So in case you notice that specific people aren't using it even as you arrive, virtually take it out.

But the alternative is not actual.

That's why the healthy is sensible. If you're in a black in shape at an advertising and marketing organization, wherein anybody wears extra cushty garments, certainly take off your jacket and tie, and this is it: you are inside the loop.

Men's Clothing for Work

The label additionally regulates guys's clothing for work.

The man have to avoid very brief pants or ties of insufficient length (lengthy or too short). Remember that the pinnacle of the tie need to cover the belt buckle. The shirts cannot be with the cuffs.

The wrong combinations also are horrible. The stocking should be the coloration of the pants or the shoe.

The brown shoe ought to be worn in moderate fits, whilst black suits with darker ones.

The tie can satisfactory be a garish coloration if the shirt is light and the healthy is dark.

Finally, the quantities need to have accurate trim (they can not be sincere or too loose). The use of extravagant belts isn't always endorsed and the jackets want no longer be completely buttoned. The remaining button can also emerge as free.

For female

For the female, it's far wonderful to stick to the traditional code, which advises modest discretion. Whether at paintings or at a right reception, a tailleur with understated tones usually works thoroughly. She need to avoid the long pants that handiest fit nicely in the internal workings and casual receptions like glad-hours, for example.

The bar of apparel or skirts ought to no longer be too short. On the out of doors, it is normally prudent to head away it underneath the knee.

Sleeveless, very short or low-reduce blouses also are inadvisable wherein there may be formality. Transparencies, immoderate glare and flashy props need to additionally be averted.

Shoes with very excessive heels want to be averted on a ordinary basis. 23

BREAKING THE ICE

Many humans tell a funny story to break the tension, however this isn't very advocated. Often the comedian story is in bad taste and even if it is not, you run the danger of now not liking it.

It is better to behave glaringly, to talk a piece bit approximately the time, the economic system, the branch in which you act and so forth. These issues help lower the preliminary anxiety. Here's how a young executive who has simply been introduced to the administrators of a business enterprise might say:

"You are very well located ... The view from the window is breathtaking." Starting the conversation like this, for smaller topics, it is less difficult to get agreement. This allows to interrupt the ice.

What we need to avoid, as we've got already pointed out, is to enter into non-public subjects. This may be very terrible, besides in situations wherein this kind of communication contributes to the purpose of the meeting.

MEETING LABEL

In the case of meetings, a few care can be taken. For instance, the period of the assembly. It is crucial to outline, every time possible, how extended the interviews will last. Normally, who need to set the time is the host. This is already performed on the starting of the verbal exchange. It isn't always loss of education. On the opposite, it's far a way of situating human beings and making the meeting more purpose.

Here is an instance of the manner to proceed:

Executive, receiving the traveler: - ... I honestly am very inquisitive about your venture ... Ah ... I booked till eleven thirty for this assembly, is it appropriate for you? "An crucial element: whoever invites or convenes the meeting is constantly the leader of the meeting. It is he who gives the route of the communique."

Punctuality

The lack of punctuality is a horrible gaffe.

We understand that once in a while it is elaborate to obtain on time because of site visitors, from a distance. But this want to be predicted on every occasion we make a date with someone.

Even worse is in case you are the host. If you invite someone for a lunch or a   commercial enterprise employer verbal exchange, you can not arrive late. You do not have that right. Of route, the put off will regularly be inevitable. So one must at the least hold professionalism and right now phone the cellular phone to inform them they will be overdue, explaining why.

That is professionalism and beauty.

cellphone gaffe The

Nothing is worse than answer the telephone throughout a assembly. It's terrible. It is rude to serve him, besides in particular instances.

Let's say the authorities goes to a assembly and his partner is within the health center. Well, if so, it is ideal to warn others that the telephone will stay related and supply an reason for why. And then most effective solution the calls that come from the sanatorium.

Other than that, the knowledgeable is to reveal off the cellular telephone. Incidentally, any form of interruption need to be prevented. If you get a person for your room, it's miles terrible to answer calls all through the conversation.

26

LABEL IN APPROVALS, lunch and dinner

with fact in which more gaffes occur are at receptions, lunches and formal dinners.

These gaffes, however, can be prevented if the authorities obeyed a few very smooth and incredible policies.

Let's get to recognize the ones tips:

Business

lunch - A company lunch must in no way exceed hours. It's the restriction. "Not too speedy, of course. A 25-minute lunch is sort of a snack, this means that it is a awful indicator. Probably the deal modified into awful.

- In a two-hour lunch, between the appetizer, the food and the dessert, there may be an average of 40 mins there. If it is a self-issuer restaurant, the time is even shorter: 1/2-hour on common. So there may be greater than an hour left to speak about industrial enterprise.

- Proper time to speak about organization is after lunch.

- A lot of humans consume and communicate about enterprise corporation on the same time. This is handiest allowed if human beings have regarded every different for a long time. There's no hassle. They every realize they have got little time, just so they waft at once to the problem, consuming and setting employer. But if it is the number one time the meeting takes place, you need to not do it.

It is the host which you need to outline while getting into organisation-related topics. It is he who says the moment, no longer the visitor.

Who Invites to Pay the Bill

Another vital recommendation: If it is a business agency lunch, the invitee can pay the bill. Unless it's miles a lunch meeting among subordinate and boss. In this situation, the boss usually pays, no matter the fact that the subordinate has referred to as the meeting. It is an issue of delicacy, due to the fact the state of affairs is artwork.

Already at the same time as a tough and speedy of pals combines a lunch, snack or dinner, the account need to be divided similarly via way of the big fashion of provides. In that case, it's miles dishonest to want to pay the bill on my own. This is a rule of etiquette.

Special care

- One should no longer ask for the maximum luxurious meals sincerely as it became invited and lunch might be paid via the enterprise. This is a fake pas.

- "Hard" dishes have to moreover be prevented. It's too terrible you order a meal and then discover you do now not like what you ordered.

- The satisfactory is to invite for reasons about the dishes for the waiter, due to the fact the same dish can be prepared in specific techniques relying on the area or united states in which you are. But in case you requested, you want to consume.

Using the Napkin

It is not uncommon for human beings to be unsure approximately a way to apply the tissue serviette in the   eating place, following the rules of etiquette. Do this:

- When you take a seat down down, the number one detail you do is positioned the napkin for your lap. If it   is starched, depart it folded horizontally via the creases simply so it does not slip.

- Whenever you deliver the glass to your mouth, first skip the serviette in your lips.

- If you need to arise from the desk during the meal, undergo in thoughts to place the napkin on the towel, to the left of the plate, with out folding it. At the give up of the meal, after the espresso, do the same.

HowtoEatChickens and Pasta

Eating fowl on the side of your fingers is lacking in etiquette.

No rely quantity how snug the table, the right detail is typically to use fork and knife. In the latter case, if exclusive human beings are not the use of cutlery and also you do not need to cause them to uncomfortable, you may take a wing or a thigh with the paper serviette and eat collectively together with your hands.

When it involves pasta, we want to do not forget the subsequent: lowering the spaghetti is a gaffe, specifically in Italian ingesting locations.

The correct problem is to roll the dough at the fork, making the rotary movement with the cutlery propped at its give up. Thus, the dough absorbs the sauce. You can also use the spoon for guide. It is held through the left hand and the fork consists of the mass to the mouth.

Drinks at organisation lunches

- In elegant, alcoholic liquids are not ordered at a organisation lunch. In a few circles, one also can even admit, as long as it's far no greater than a single serving or glass of wine or an appetizer. And but, whoever want to endorse the drink is the only who invited.

- The host is what devices whether or not or no longer lunch must have alcohol or now not. The vacationer ought to in no way ask. The equal goes for cigarettes.

Picking up the chair

In a eating place, while a person gets up, one want to now not push the chair in the direction of the desk. This challenge belongs to the waiter.

But if the meal is in a residence and there can be no waiter or waitress, then positive, you need to placed it lower again in area.

Gratuities inside the restaurant

A tip is a way of expressing a thanks for pinnacle company supplied and no longer an duty.

- In the restaurant, the primary component you need to do in advance than giving a tip to the waiter is to check if the bill consists of the corporation fee.

- If you do no longer fee, you should provide 10% if the corporation modified into less expensive, 12.Five% if the provider changed into outstanding and 15% if it modified into an uncommon issuer. It's the

exercise.

- If the enterprise fee is charged, no tip is needed. However, you could supply the waiter a small quantity as a token of appreciation. Surely the waiter will recall that next time.

"In receptions (reliable or now not) or dinners in houses, underneath no times tip the waiter, no matter how discreet this courtesy." 30

Chapter 17: Receiving At Home

Every right host follows the rules with a number of situation.

- First, he and the spouse, if any, should be organized half of-hour earlier. And the whole lot have to be simply prepared to welcome the guests.

- The gadgets, like bonbons that the host gets, want to be served to the alternative site visitors. In the case of wine, the bottle may be reserved.

- The vegetation need to be located in pots without delay and prominently in the residence.

- The hosts flow into all of the time, amongst their visitors, introducing each other and leaving them relaxed.

Late dinners

- The visitor need to attain among half of an hour earlier than and 15 mins after the scheduled time. Getting to the vicinity out of doors this range is rude. So ship the label. After this tolerance of 15 minutes, the host has the table served.

 - It ought to be taken into consideration, but, that any put off, even of first-class 5 minutes, is a lack of interest.

- Upon arrival, the latecomer need to apologize to surely all and sundry present for delaying the meal. If the 15 mins of tolerance were exhausted and dinner has began, the latecomer is served from the dish this is on the desk inside the meanwhile.

 - If they'll be already within the dessert, the host will visit the kitchen and make a dish with what changed into the principle meals.

Places marked the desk

In formal dinners, it is commonsee playing cards on the table putting ahead who sits in which. This is part of the easy protocol that is observed through top executives and distant places personalities.

Tradition says that the traveler of honor - who isn't always the individual for whom the ceremonial dinner is being given however as an alternative someone of excessive rank - should sit to the proper of the host, and the human beings of inferior feature, seated in order decreasing alongside the desk.

"But you need to look ahead to the host's sign to name the traffic to the table. Do now not pass taking the first vacant vicinity you find.

- Wait for the host to point in that you want to take a seat, and endure in mind not to take too lengthy to reply the decision.

- If there aren't any call playing playing cards at the desk, and the host does not designate in which the site visitors should sit down, you may choose wherein you may sit down, but you need to excuse folks that are already seated.

- It is right to take a look at that chair with backrest towards the table suggests that the area is reserved.

Pre-Dinner Drinks

If you will serve pre-dinner beverages and canapés, schedule the start of the meal for approximately an hour after the time detailed inside the invitation. They can be served at a bar counter, at buffet tables or on trays brought by the use of manner of waiters.

If the beverages aren't part of the plan, but although served, you have to wait about twenty mins to start serving the food.

This provision, even, may be very not unusual whilst one of the visitors is overdue. regarding a few policies of etiquette could make a distinction.

Some of those policies relate to manners and refinement, others to the way you relate to the ones round you. Here are some indispensable precautions:

- Never lie down at the chair or lean over the plate you'll eat. Instead, live tuned and show self notion.

- If you have got were given been invited, do not bitch about the meals or the carrier. Leave any feedback about it on behalf of the host.

"Good manners tell you to chew in silence." To facilitate, reduce small portions of food and chew them with closed mouth. Do no longer drink a few issue at the same time as your mouth is entire. Chewing the ice on the drinks isn't always pinnacle both.

"The desk, in no manner stretch your arm to get whatever that is a methods from you. Only use what's close to you.

Moderation is the entirety. You may additionally even drink a couple of serving as extended because the host moreover does so and invite you to do the same. However, in no way pass the 2nd dose. The rule is likewise valid in case you are the host: no longer some thing extra than doses.

"Sit at the table, do now not flip your gaze to exceptional tables, noticing who's going in or out. Your hobby want to be directed completely to the ones at your table.

- If you have were given been invited, anticipate the host to begin consuming and accompany. Try to act similar to him, respecting, of path, the boundaries of common sense.

- No combing or straightening hair at the table. Women ought to additionally now not brush up their make-up at the same time as they're seated.

- In the front of others, do not use toothpicks or floss at any time. It is also a terrible gaffe to easy tooth with the tongue on the quit of the meal.

- When you finish ingesting, go away the dish exactly in that you're. Pushing the plate earlier is an unforgivable rudeness.

Using cutlery

Manipulation of cutlery works as a sort of communication code to the waiter. See:

- In any installing which lunch or dinner takes location - whether in a eating place or someone's domestic - you may advocate that the dish may be removed with the aid of the use of leaving the fork and knife facet thru factor on the proper side at the plate.

- In the United States, it's far an super concept to maintain your fork prongs up; in Europe, down.

- However, if you have to prevent for a few moments to be privy to someone, bypass the knife and fork, along with your teeth down, on the plate. This is a signal which you aren't finished but.

Behavior inside the presence of the waiter

At a eating place desk, if the waiter arrives and the hassle you are speaking approximately is reserved, the nice element to do is to prevent talking at the same time as the meal is served. By the time the waiter requests go away to serve, the purchaser need to lean again barely leaving a free area. You should thank in a low voice.

How to make a toast

- In formal situations, at the time of the toast, really enhance the glass or the cup after the person makes the toast.

- In intimate conferences, it is well well really worth touching the glass lightly at the those who are closer, or on all if you want. Saying "tintim" is a part of the toast!

- It is crucial to bear in mind that, in any situation, you handiest start to drink after the toast has been made.

- Once the toast is made, it is compulsory that the person drinks a number of the drink and does now not positioned the glass on the desk with out ingesting.

Practical Form of Toasting

If it's as much as you to make the toast, be excellent, but speedy and intention. Long speeches are tiring and, moreover, you always run the danger of appearing pretentious or at least stressful.

Here's an instance of the manner to toast a friend:

"- To Diego! And might also moreover success usually be an partner to your exceptional talents!"

That's enough.

How to pay the bill

1 - The host need to pay the invoice.

2 - He ought to tell the maitre, formerly, that the account must be introduced in his hands.

3 - If you probably did not tell the maitre d, at the time of requesting the bill positioned your credit score rating card subsequent in your plate as a signal. And keep the account away from the visible form of your site visitors.

At the quit of the meal

An informed host continues a be careful for the traffic until the very last minute. It is really useful to accompany them to the door and, if vital, to the car after they depart.

At this moment, the host need to thank the traveler and, taking gain of the opportunity, every can change gambling cards or schedule a present day assembly.

MORE SIGNS ABOUT DINING AND RECEPTION LABEL

The following suggestions serve both the host and the visitor:

- In a eating place, in case you have been the handiest who invited, in advance than ordering the dishes or the wine, ask the guests within the event that they they do not need to signify something. That's precise.

- When you're invited to someone's domestic, ship vegetation or deliver a box of sweets.

- If you are touring to China or Japan, learn how to consume with the hashi pair.

- Outside, or perhaps in the u.S. Of america, if at the lunch for which an invited dish is served an unknown dish, devour even without liking. And do now not are looking for to understand what is completed.

"It's no longer right to take advantage of loose consultations with a scientific physician at the birthday celebration.

- If you entertain unsightly scenes (no man or woman is evidence towards this), the traveller should withdraw discreetly after apologizing to the hosts.

"Likewise, in case you want to move away early, just discretely go away the residence."

- No visitor must convey friends with out first asking if he can, and have to best reap this if he is sure that such someone will in form properly.

"Another element the visitor desires to have is" mistrust. " If you be conscious signs and signs of weariness of the hosts, you ought to mention good-bye and retire, now not forgetting to thank the invitation and reward the nice of the reception.

"The next day, we constantly call and greet the hosts for the birthday celebration. So ship the label.

At the prevent of this financial disaster, here is a tip that continuously works:

37

Being invited to lunch or dinner, constantly "take the equal fork" due to the fact the host, ie study how he behaves and take a look at his instance. It constantly works! 38

LABEL FOR OTHER OCCASIONSGoing In the theater

to the theater, even though the show isn't gala, calls for unique care. Even for a count of recognize to the actors, put on your fine paintings clothes, even positive you will be surrounded with the resource of denims and sweatshirts everywhere in the place. You have to display which you apprehend the difference amongst a theater night time time and a soccer suit.

Remember also that the noise of bullets and bonbons being unwrapped in the direction of the session, debauch the fashion of any executive.

How to build up objects at activities

Many humans pick out to maintain birthday parties at nightclubs, restaurants or buffets.

- In this situation, the birthday boy want to welcome all of the site visitors the on the spot they arrive, thanking the objects received and that need to be opened later.

- It is critical to continually emerge as aware of the folks that gave every present. This can be very useful so as to thank over the phone or the primary possibility to locate them.

- Nothing, however, prevents the mother, relative or intimate buddy from receiving the website site visitors on the door, and may even benefit the gadgets and maintain them at the same time as the birthday boy circulates across the room.

39

How thank this

Usually the person giving a gift is stressful to understand changed into pleased to pick out and what emerge as the personreaction.

Therefore, thanking a gift properly is a sign of etiquette and schooling.

In the number one area, it isn't crucial to mention what grow to be obtained, simply thank the gesture and not the content material. Instead of pronouncing "thanks for the bracelet", it's miles far   better to mention "I simply enjoyed your gift".

Acting in this way, in addition to demonstrating the delicacy, you may additionally be   reaffirming your interest, apprehend and affection for who provided you.

Wedding Etiquette Wedding

ceremonies have formalities that cannot be disregarded, and need to be discovered exactly as directed by using the use of the etiquette.

- Invitations, as an instance, ought to be introduced to visitors at the least 30 days in improve. That way, you are ensuring human beings do not make one-of-a-kind commitments via the identical date.

- A approach broadly used in invitations is the printing of phrases which includes "the bride and groom will gain greetings in the church". But that is very inelegant.

- If the reception is restricted best to family people and extra intimate humans, they ought to get maintain of a in addition invitation to be placed in the envelope.

- When receiving greetings from the vestry, the couple have to be positioned between parents and grandparents. Guests additionally want to illustrate pinnacle judgment and avoid prolonged, tiring greetings. Only a few phrases of congratulations are already fulfilled. If the opposite family participants aren't diagnosed, they want to be greeted with a moderate nod.

- After receiving items and flora on the reception, the bride and groom or dad and mom need to in my view thank each visitor. However, it's far goodto report the thanks thru mail, after the give up of the

40

 honeymoon

Lately, many newlyweds choose out to ask 3 or more sponsor couples. It is   an fashionable custom and a nice way to pay homage to a bigger type of cherished ones. The label accepts or maybe recommends this.

Aircraft label

- Check in on the time of test-in to make certain the carry-on baggage is the right period to maintain internal.

- During the journey, without a doubt leave the seat to visit the relaxation room.

- Avoid asking one of a kind passengers to trade locations. The accurate detail is to ask the adventure business agency enterprise for the tickets to be marked in seats next to their companions.

- If you want to talk for your neighbor within the armchair, see if he suggests hobby in chatting. If the solutions are harsh and brief, prevent the chat.

- At the time of the meal, truly open the applications of food you will consume. This prevents dirt and mess.

- Utensils that can be used whilst travelling, inclusive of toothbrushes, combs and hair brushes, want to be placed in a bag and no longer inside the bag. This avoids the trouble of setting up luggage.

- Do now not overdo alcohol. At altitude, alcohol has the best effect at the frame.

- Do no longer smoke in any respect in the bathrooms. It is a actual attack on the safety of all passengers.

- Cell phones ought to be disconnected right away upon getting into the plane. Check with commissioners if and on the identical time as you can use walkmans and notebooks.

Receiving site traffic at domestic

Send the label, to invite a person to staying in

on the Academies

The gym membership calls for some behavioral pointers:

- Never exceed the favored time limits on device with confined time.

- The weights and one-of-a-kind tool used want to be replaced in right places after use.

- Always use a material moistened with alcohol (or disinfectant that the gyms themselves make to be had) on the seats and backrests of the device after the workout is completed.

- Turn off the cellphone each time you start exercise. If it's miles important to serve you, please reap this in a reserved location.

- Review the devices and machine with which you moreover need to apply them.

- Although many people assume that gym is an area for flirting, the label only tells you to talk or chat with whoever is receptive.

- Remember that it isn't an fantastic concept to reserve a place within the gymnasium system. If it is so crucial to you, come early to beauty.

Label on the elevator

- In the elevators, the character have to continually hold the door to the doorway of the woman. Similarly, the elderly have the choice.

- If people go downstairs at the identical floor, the man or woman or the youngest man or woman must open the door for the lady or the older person to get out of the elevator.

- In business enterprise lifts, the individual have to input after the lady and allow the passage simply so she leaves first. If the bring is too complete and this delicacy is uncomfortable for human beings, the individual want to excuse himself and leave first.

- Anyone entering the elevator should greet the ones already interior.

- Conversations inner lifts should be prevented. Unless you are on my own with a chaperone.

Ladder label

When descending a ladder, the gentleman need to constantly flow inside the the the front. When mountain climbing, the female should have a look at within the front of the gentleman. If you're aged collectively with you, provide to take the briefcase or programs she or he is wearing.

Smoking label

Smokers want to take precautions earlier than lights a cigarette in an unusual enclosure, particularly if it's far a house.

It is crucial to ensure if there is an ashtray inside the residence or if someone is smoking. If there may be no such proof, it's far amazing not to moderate the cigarette. It is exceptional to ask permission from the belongings owner first. You can ask and experience how the owners of the house reply.

Label at the seaside

- Your song may be your fine corporation employer but for others it could not be. Preferably, pay attention to your walkman, discman or radio with earphones. If you do now not have a headset and you need to take note of the radio, do no longer scream it. If you need to pay interest tune screaming, pass away from special people.

- The rule is straightforward: in case you're going to play coolbol or some component, stay away from unique humans. Stay in a safety zone that doesn't endanger the integrity of special bathers. Do now not take delivery of as real at the side of your functionality. Rely on commonplace revel in.

- Get away from humans if you want to shake off your towel and, specifically, see which aspect the wind blows while shaking it. Remember that sands are like phrases: taken by using using the wind.

- Do now not absorb greater region than critical. When you get to the beach, does no longer begin to spreadbags,sandalsandtowelsaroundtheareaa roundyou,asif

you have got been the owner of the seashore. Contain your self in a space that must be your towel plus some thing else for the junk.

- Even if the seashore is crowded, try no longer to get too close to great people and do no longer talk to friends besides you're an acquaintance. You can smile at the same time as you arrive, however now not anything more. Although the beach is a place of relaxation, be discreet.

Did you forget a person's name?

It occurs to definitely absolutely everyone. Sometimes we forget about the call of the person we sincerely met, do no longer we? So, what to do right now?

The great element to do is be honest, express regret and ask in kindly "What's your call over again?" after which preserve the verbal exchange.

Other humans motel to extremely good forms of belongings, collectively with:

"Sorry, what's your entire name anyway?"

"Oh, excuse me, as you even spell your call, I would really like to write down down down your cellular phone clearly so we meet again ..."

Among numerous excuses, use some element you decide on, but commonly be type and show interest in character.

Visiting sufferers

- Only go to sufferers when you have data from circle of relatives or clinical employees that the affected person is launched.

- If you want the man or woman to recognise that you've been to the hospital - despite the truth that you have not been allowed in - go away a enterprise business organisation card to your behalf and characteristic the nurse supply it to you as rapid as viable.

- If you go to a affected individual on your own home, call beforehand, and time table an appointment with the subsequent of family. Never appear with the beneficial useful resource of marvel.

APPENDIX I LABEL IN MOUNT CURRICULUM

The curricula are posted with the useful resource of which a system seeker offers - atdistance

- for opinions. That is why care have to be even greater.

Here are a few recommendations on a way to set up your resume in a realistic and green manner, conveying a excellent picture that does not enhance doubts approximately your personality and information.

1. The textual content need to be clean, with the great Portuguese, precise records and without ambivalence or dubiety of interpretations.

2. Avoid writing within the first person singular, "I did," "I befell," and lots of others. This can cause an effect of arrogance and vanity. Also keep away from adjectives and use extra nouns, in which feasible with concrete numbers. If critical, use the help of books or magazines.

three. The curriculum should don't have any a whole lot much less than one and a maximum of 3 to four   pages. If your expert experience or educational research are very big, summarize the number one topics. Tip: Add a cover letter because the primary net web page.

4. Personal statistics must be positioned at the number one page, or first web page (which isn't the quilt letter). Simply positioned the entire name, age, marital fame, numbers of kids or dependents. If you have got got had been given citizenship it is vital to mention. Do no longer forget about approximately about the complete cope with, cellphone, mobile and e mail.

 5. Be clean and purpose about the purpose of sending your resume and thing out the supposed function and the chosen area.

6. Do no longer waste space telling you wherein to take the immoderate school or high college route. Just do it, of path, in case you are getting into the project market. Focus

extra on vocational, undergraduate, postgraduate or sturdy point courses that you do not forget maximum applicable.

7. It could be very vital which you understand one or extra languages, ideally

English and Spanish, however do no longer say what you do not understand. If best writes or fine nicely talking locations language, be sincere. Knowledge of foreign languages isn't always generally important.

eight. Mention obtained professional revel in. Tell in that you labored, positions held, period of carrier, and so on. If you have got unique facts, quote as nicely.

9. The professional trajectory need to be stated at the number one page, genuinely beneath your personal data, simply so a easy appearance from the reader allows you to realise and take a look at its trajectory.

10. Some say that profits need to not be referred to in a curriculum as it turns into a possible barrier. But there are businesses that

want to streamline. Therefore, this item is on the discretion of each one.

Important Remarks

- Do no longer deliver pictures to the curriculum till requested.

- It is right, in advance than sending the curriculum, that a few buddy or professional professional analyzes. You can also want to make a few safety.

- People with bodily disabilities have to say in their curriculum what type of incapacity they have got. So you may be heading off a probable embarrassment, due to the reality there are though groups that cultivate a powerful prejudice about it.

APPENDIX 2 CONDUCTING CONVERSATIONS NICE

The paintings of communique is a information that may be placed, practiced and perfected even the maximum timid. Everything is a matter of rest and steering.

- Learn to triumph over the limits that frequently take region in lengthy conversations. Shame, lack of confidence, nervousness, language problems and diction may be minimized via have a examine, training, or maybe remedy.

- Enrich your problem rely for conversations. Current occasions, movies and books, gastronomy and ingesting locations, song, human psychology and pursuits are wealthy resources. At least on this kind of topics try and delve deeper.

- Practice the paintings of talking to humans you agree with. Try new topics, new techniques of speaking or even improvisations all through the verbal exchange.

- Be properly informed. Read newspapers, magazines, books, watch new tv indicates.

- Try to move deeper into subjects of interest to humans near you and workout speaking about them.

- Learn some early terms like, "You understand, the opportunity day I observed out that the wide variety of vehicle fatalities in Brazil in a three hundred and sixty five days is more than the whole Vietnam War?" Or "You Did you notice the final normal overall performance of that play? "

Ask questions for others who will help the verbal exchange to flow. "Is it real that doctors generally hate writing?" or "Do you discovered a disarmament marketing campaign is wanted in Brazil?"

- Show interest within the verbal exchange, with eyes, ears and mind vast open for what's being referred to. Show yourself stunned, satisfied, or stimulated with the terms.

- Tryread the reactions of humans round them and from themfits

 your conversation.

- Many humans like to talk about pets, meals, decor, houses, movie stars and TV, soccer.

145

Most do no longer like to speak about wages, politics, faith, or pc structures. But that could be a generalization that isn't valid on high excellent activities.

Chapter18: Meaning Of Netiquette

This word have turn out to be first of all popularized in postings of the satirical "Dear Emily" news columns in 1983, although it started out in advance than the World Wide Web. In that duration, the economic utilization of public posting have become now not common and net traffic have become ruled with the resource of the usage of textual content-primarily based emails, Gopher, Telnet, and FTP from academic and studies our our bodies.

Although the particular guidelines regulating netiquette can be severa counting on the forum getting used, it is further applicable to chatting, walking a blog, message boards, e mail, and surfing the Internet.

The terms community and etiquette and is described as a machine of norms for appropriate online hobby. Similarly, on-line ethics specializes within the permissible use of net assets in an internet social placing.

Both terms are often interchanged and are regularly blended with the concept of a 'netizen' which itself is a contraction of the phrases internet and citizen and refers to each a person who uses the internet to take part in society and an man or woman who has regular the duty of the usage of the internet in effective and socially accountable techniques.

Netiquette is a gadget of hints that permits proper on line behavior referring to the social and cultural norms of a set. These norms can trade based totally mostly on the environment/context (casual/formal), women and men (acquainted/surprising with every distinctive), interest, and form of era hired. Noncompliance with netiquette guidelines is probably taken into consideration as a display of disrespect.

Why are we able to Need Netiquette Rules?

The norms of decorum that observe on the identical time as interacting online are extraordinary from those who follow at the same time as speaking in character. It can not be anticipated that youngsters inherently understand a way to speak in an internet context. Netiquette necessities have arisen to allow on-line interactions within the lack of seen and audible clues, which may also frequently reason misunderstandings considering readers can and now not the usage of a hassle misread communications.

Knowledge of community etiquette inhibits incorrect online interest and warfare of phrases. Class interactions the use of netiquette boom social connections, community formation, and take delivery of as actual with amongst participants. It encourages a steady, attractive, well mannered, and collaborative organization wherein quite some reviews is valued.

Why Should I Incorporate Netiquette Rules in my Online Course?

You are advised to feature a thing on netiquette on your on-line direction syllabus to decorate attention of its relevance.

Netiquette may additionally help college students to decorate their mild skills, lessen miscommunications, assist students better draw close what is socially proper at the same time as jogging and cooperating online in severa situations, and guarantee that the teaching and reading manner isn't impeded. Netiquette pointers can encourage professional necessities of conduct within the online placing, as required inside the conventional study room.

Chapter 19: Types Of Netiquette

To describe first-rate netiquettes, it is important to first differentiate between sorts of communique.

Netiquette is generally generated from the first form of conversation and then applies with modest modifications for publicly accessible debates and dialogues.

One-to-one communique: Emails, personal messaging in unique mediums.

One-to-many communique: Mailing lists, public chats, forums, pin boards, WWW forums, social networks, agencies, net net sites, and microblogging offerings.

Moreover, a difference also can be installed amongst business business enterprise communication (B2B, B2C) and personal talks, wherein similar behavioral standards are followed, which may be complemented through agency inner and agency hints.

There are severa behavioral necessities on the Internet.

Each netiquette is reliant at the virtual media, the relevant internet web page operator, or provider company and can have specific regulations.

Here are some instances of numerous virtual media and for my part decided norms of conduct.

E-mails, mailing lists, newsletters:

Greetings, a courteous cope with, similarly to a exquisite spelling of the carried out phrases and terms are a call for.

The receiver need to be politely welcomed and spoken good-bye to.

The substance of the e-mail need to be clean and intelligible and must be conveyed via a concise difficulty line.

Due to terrific individual gadgets and obstacles in e-mail conversation, it is also advised to make use of elegant individual encodings collectively with ASCII or Unicode.

Very large attachments are allotted with out of regard for the receiver and their Internet connection.

Spam emails are regularly visible as a breach of netiquette.

Forums, chats, and communities: Chats (chatiquette), forums, and organizations commonly be privy to courteous remedy and proper technical utilization.

The contributors ought to not insult an extra and all verbal exchange must take place in step with the policies of the technological medium.

Courtesy, further to factually appropriate topics and the avoidance of flow-posts and multiple postings.

Extensive utilization of capital is deemed yelling and the clarity leaves a bargain to be desired.

Greeting and parting expressions are as vital as unique spelling.

In many sorts of media, however, specific terminology and abbreviations have grown acquainted, which constitute troubles for laymen and novices.

Wikis and translations help.

Social media and microblogging: In social networks, collectively with Facebook and microblogging offerings together with Twitter, netiquettes are important to save you insulting, racist, and sexist feedback further to cyber-mobbing and stalking.

Through the virtual conversation form, some customers are frequently tempted to transgress the boundaries of traditional communique.

Shit-storms regularly bring about and in component even legally applicable derailments, which not pleasant violate the policies of use of the respective medium but furthermore breach the overall requirements of netiquettes.

Participants are suggested to be courteous and to conform with the phrases of use and hints, which may be regularly ideal to the medium.

Practical relevance reference and criminal issues

In virtual media, however, this consists of now not clearly being courteous however additionally respecting elements together with statistics safety, privateness, safety necessities, or copyright and use rights.

Indeed, netiquette and its enforcement regions are in the hands of the operator of a medium, but first rate infractions of hints may additionally moreover moreover result in prison violations which pass a long manner beyond interpersonal norms and constitute fines.

A breach of netiquette is generally adversely sanctioned, for example, through the use of the worried discussion board member receiving a caution or the sender of an e-mail being knowledgeable approximately the violation of netiquette.

In the occasion of criminal infringements, such consequences may be significantly greater massive.

Netiquette is regularly taken into consideration nonbinding, despite the fact that some infractions of the thoughts of the unification can also bring about criminal offenses and the dividing strains are regularly blurry.

Examples encompass shit-storms, which encompass hate speech and agitation, or the importing of a included paintings that disregards copyright and use rights.

In workout, there were severa criminal transgressions in current some years, that have led to fines and went properly past terrible punishments.

Relevance to usability

Netiquettes are meant to streamline human interactions and provide binding norms for all clients in a verbal exchange medium.

This now not handiest issues troubles consisting of etiquette, language, or clarity, but moreover the realistic usage of digital media.

Aspects at the side of facts safety, privateness, protection, and a huge sort of regulation in the sphere of the media may be handled through netiquettes, preferred terms and conditions, terms of use, and self-obvious conduct in communique.

Often, those norms emerge slowly in the utilization of the medium (they are added thru the net web site proprietors.

From the thing of view of ⅝ media, netiquettes are because of this an inherent aspect of the usage of such media at the internet, social internet, or the semantic net.

Chapter 20: Basic Rules Of Netiquette

Remember to address human beings the manner they want to be handled.

Introduce your self and politely approach to them; use their name.

Use emoticons sparingly to assist specific tone at the same time as speaking in masses much less formal contexts.

Try now not to harm people's sentiments or create offense.

Avoid utilization of All CAPS, considering that you could look to be yelling.

Consider extraordinary's gender and cultural variations; keep away from gender and cultural jokes and sarcasm.

Behave Ethically and Responsibly:

Think earlier than pushing the deliver button – recall your message is everlasting.

Act inner conventional cultural requirements.

Respect Internet lawsprivacy,

intellectual assets and copyright guidelines.

Credit special's efforts

Complete activity on time.

Familiarize Yourself with the Technology and Environment:

Familiarize oneself with severa social and cultural conventions.

Recognize that high quality situations could require a one-of-a-type amount of ritual than others.

Recognize that numerous strategies can also furthermore demand exquisite netiquette norms.

Lurk earlier than you soar. Familiarize yourself; then be a part of in.

Respect Others Time and Bandwidth:

Make contributions succinct, applicable, and insightful.

Don't dominate debates.

Recognize that others should have high-quality issues.

Don't assume fast replies or for every person to pay attention in your efforts.

Restrict emails/postings to direction-relevant content material fabric by myself.

Present Yourself Positively:

Become knowledgeable approximately your mission.

Write in a smooth, orderly, logical, and accurate fashion.

Run a quick spell test; it suggests professionalism.

Be kind and courteous; useful resource others anyplace possible.

Respect others' numerous mind and viewpoints.

Share Your Knowledge and Expertise,

Contribute and percentage online:

Be conscious that sharing information online is positivesit fosters communicate and knowledge improvement.

It permits growth take into account and an internet network.

Keep Flame Wars underneath Control:

Recognize that Netiquette prevents "flame wars" that dominate the tone and undermine the camaraderie of a forum.

Avoid using unsightly and antagonistic terms; no bullying.

Online conversations must be nice.

Seek explanation beforehand, for the reason that fabric can also have been misconstrued.

Be Forgiving of Others' Mistakes:

Be forgiving — there will continuously be new on-line freshmen.

Be forgiving if someone makes a mistake.

Be respectful on the identical time as notifying someone of an etiquette hassle; use private e-mail.

Remember that anybody make errors; have tolerance.

Course Communications

Make the degree of ritual obvious!

There are severa device and locations for interacting online. Distinct online situations may also moreover name for one among a type Netiquette norms. Although university college students may be pretty used to interacting informally in social forums, the expectancies and norms for an educational context can be pretty unique. Therefore you must create easy standards for the amount of formality and writing style which you would possibly want to search for your path.

More Formal?

If your aim is to foster robust writing competencies, then it's miles going to be crucial for scholars to study appropriate writing norms regarding spelling, grammar, and punctuation. For example, you could need students to utilize a positive writing style, which incorporates APA or MLA, and to assist their arguments with right mentioning.

Less Formal?

However, if your aim is to preserve language in particular unfastened and conversational, then emoticons, acronyms, slang, and so forth. May be high-quality.

Discussion and Group boards may also additionally moreover variety—they may be particularly dependable or quite casual in tone, depending upon their cause and the difficulty being addressed. Virtual environments that sell interaction or content cloth manufacturing such as blogs, wikis, live training, or particular social networking sites (Facebook, Twitter, and so on.) regularly foster a extra casual placing.

Chapter 21: Netiquette Examples

Netiquette requirements decorate social interactions, community development, and consider and assist set up a steady, appealing, polite, and collaborative environment in which diversity of opinion is recommended.

Example 1

Course Expectations (Discussions — Formal)

Participation on this course will shape a big amount of your grade. In this direction, we're capable of be speaking every week the usage of on-line conversations. It is expected that the communique might be respectful of Netiquette Rules and mirror the very best necessities of professional speak. This does no longer recommend which you can not specific competing reviews. You are endorsed to speak about a in addition's opinions and foster appealing dialogues. However, unprofessional and disrespectful comments (pointless blazing and flame wars), like in the real take a look at room, have to be averted online. Your writing is expected to be formal using suitable grammar, punctuation, and spelling. Please adhere to strict APA formatting and offer references to help your ideas. Slang, abbreviations, and emoticons are not appropriate.

Any posting that does not seem to paste to professional necessities may be eliminated. In such a case, it's going to possibly be the duty of the pupil to offer a alternative posting to fulfill route necessities.

Example 2

Course Expectations (Discussions — Informal)

Participation on this direction is essential to assist useful resource your route readings. We might be speakme each week via online conversations. It is anticipated that communicate may be respectful to Netiquette Rules. This does not imply which you can't express competing critiques. You are recommended to talk approximately but any other's evaluations and foster engaging dialogues. However, unprofessional and disrespectful remarks (unnecessary blazing and flame wars), like within the actual look at room, have to be avoided on-line. Conversations are purported to be short and conversational. Please be conscious that THE USE OF ALL CAPS CAN MAKE IT LOOK LIKE YOU ARE SHOUTING on line and should be averted. The strategic use of emoticons is usually recommended to assist in talking tone or emotion this is hard to determine on line.

Please be well mannered and try and make all communications smooth.

Example 3

Course Expectations (Twitter Communications — Informal)

Participation on this direction includes installing region a Twitter Account and Tweeting to your classmates every week on given topics thru the Twitter widget, displayed to your Course Home internet page. It is anticipated that every Tweet may be respectful of Netiquette Rules. Remember,

Twitter confines your message to a most of 280 characters (which includes the hashtag), so these Tweets are expected to be rather brief, focused, and succinct! All Tweets are supposed to be surprisingly casual. Abbreviation and emoticon utilization is recommended.

Chapter 22: Netiquette And Society

Recognizing that the net is an extension of society. The net isn't a modern-day universe in which the whole thing is going, but instead, a today's measurement of the fact around us.

Applying the equal necessities on-line as we do in public. In easy phrases, due to this the necessities society has in location towards hate speech and intolerance, infant exploitation, toddler pornography, copyright breaches, and first rate forms of theft, stay intact. Values of decency, kindness, transparency, and treating people with the equal respect we preference to collect need to additionally be adhered to.

Refusing to assist abuse and harassment on the equal time as on-line. Accepting that the legal guidelines which are now in region to defend the rights and dignity of humans study on line and that when suitable, regulation is modified to mirror the ones rights inside the increased context. Theft, harassment, and bullying even as online are although theft, harassment, and bullying, period.

Acknowledging cultural differences. Even at the same time as national traces not exist, cultural admire and tolerance should persist. This consists of locating a way to understand that the social values and norms of high-quality netizens will no longer be the social values and norms of all netizens.

Chapter 23: Business Netiquette

For organizations, being an extraordinary netizen, adopting online ethics, and using netiquette consist of:

Respecting rights of privacy for offline employees. Information owned through human beings in their offline contacts need to be expert.

Maintaining openness in information insurance. By taking movement in order that customers can without issues and short recognize how that enterprise organisation is using their records and shielding them from harm, groups can provide customers with a easy manner of ownership and self-strength of mind as to what is, and isn't shared approximately them, which strengthens the customer courting.

Internet etiquette or netiquette is surely expert and social sports activities which might be judged right on line. This way being kind and respectful to every body you encounter, the equal way you need to inside the head to head discussions. It additionally consists of gadgets that are not precisely relevant in actual-lifestyles settings but are even though vast in actual-life corporation duties and relationships.

Netiquette is vital within the equal manner that essential politeness is vital. Your net behaviors may replicate on you and your commercial enterprise business enterprise regardless of how a fantastic deal it deviates from the way you portray your self in person.

Anything you put up or transmit on-line additionally leaves a digital footprint that is probably traced yet again to you. Netiquette is essential in jogging a enterprise enterprise; one wrong submit in your social media internet web page or one sick-counseled email despatched to an investor or ability client need to signal the harm of your business employer or as a minimum tarnish the recognition you labored so tough to increase.

A business's fulfillment isn't always just judged with the aid of approaches effectively you deliver the gadgets or services as promised, but by way of manner of the manner you have interaction with all the parents which is probably without delay or no longer without delay associated with your enterprise – from ends in customers to buyers to humans. The ties you make with those people may want to probably favorably or adversely affect your corporation operation.

As the leader of the business enterprise, handling the industrial business enterprise, searching over operations, and certifying outputs, your plate is virtually constantly complete. You don't have the steeply-priced to sit down and communicate at the side of your colleagues or to in my opinion thank your customers and clients. The right news is that there are now precise channels of communication, numerous which might be on-line. With this in thoughts, it's vital to behave professionally in some unspecified time in the future of all your internet structures.

Here are three key useful outcomes for your commercial enterprise corporation while you pick to continuously have a look at appropriate netiquette.

1. Genuine Partnership

As previously stated, your reference to the human beings you do business commercial enterprise business enterprise with is critical. By no longer being ugly, in-man or woman, or on-line, you get to create deep and actual connections. Not that you need to expect some component in go back, but parents are greater inclined to offer decrease once more to folks who've validated them compassion. Choose to be superb, constantly.

For example, by way of way of manner of filtering your thoughts in desire to in reality getting into online what goes into your thoughts, you block any ugly words that would drastically have an effect in your connection with the people on that channel.

2. Strong Credibility

By obeying name or e mail ethics, or whatever online systems you hire, you generate a incredible photo now not only for your self, however in your employer as properly. When you're constantly careful and sympathetic, you show the great professionalism that ultimately creates and reinforces credibility. Then in case you're first rate enough, do not forget in fact pours out organically from others.

3. Decrease In Miscommunication

With your annoying time desk, it's low cost that you could't find the cash for to move throughout the bush at the same time as speakme. However, you want to be cautious for the purpose that there's a narrow line among being direct and being unpleasant or immodest. Due to the lack of body language, false impression is a set up trouble even as the use of digital verbal exchange techniques like texting and email. The very last element you want is to upset or piss off the ones you are working tough to acquire out to.

Proper etiquette have to be decided on all on line structures and devices along side social media, net boards, emails, laptops, texting, and further. It usually will pay to make a planned attempt to be kind and courteous in all your transactions on line thinking about the fact that some thing you write or the e-mail may additionally additionally thoroughly come lower again to grasp-out you. In the end, all of it comes proper right down to recognize - recognize for others and apprehend for your self and all you've labored difficult for.

Whatever virtual tool you use, textual verbal exchange in the shape of short messages, or texting, has turn out to be a wellknown method to have interaction. It is extremely good for brief conversations, and is a practical approach to hold related with folks at the same time as speakme on the smartphone might be burdensome. Texting is not useful for lengthy or sophisticated communications, and due idea should take shipping of to the audience.

It is sometimes believed that you could tell how vintage a person is through how he or she types a cellphone quantity on a mobile cellphone. If the character makes use of his or her thumb even as conserving the virtual tool, that man or woman can also moreover had been reared on video video video games and be professional at one-exceeded interfaces. If he holds the digital device with one hand and enters the range with the possibility, he may be over thirty, and probably be much less snug with certain cutting-edge device. Of reality, there may be no real link among enter and age, but it's far a beneficial instance to make use of at the same time as thinking about who your target audience is on the same time as sending a textual content message. If the person is a one-hader and is privy to all of the abbreviations common to texting, you will be in a position to utilize similar codes to speak efficiently. If the character is a -hander, you're higher off using fewer terms and spelling them out. Texting may be a top notch technique for interacting even as on the road, however recollect your target marketplace and your agency, and use phrases, key terms, or abbreviations for you to supply your message.

Tips for Effective Business Texting

Know your receiver; "dsct" be an affordable way to invite a close to accomplice what the proper bargain is to offer a particular client, however in case you are sending a textual content for your boss, it is able to be ultimate to country, "what % bargain does Murray get on $1K order?"

Anticipate inadvertent false impression. Texting usually includes symbols and codes to hold thoughts, thoughts, and emotions. Given the complexity of communication, and the valuable but constrained tool of texting, take heed to its restrict and decrease false impression with brief texts.

Contacting a person too regularly might probably border on harassment. Texting is a device. Use it whilst appropriate however don't overuse it.

Unplug your self on occasion. Do you usually feel linked? Do you enjoy out of place or "out of it" in case you don't have your cellular cell smartphone and can not connect with others, even for fifteen minutes? Sometimes being unreachable for some time may be healthful—the whole lot carefully, even texting.

Don't text and energy. Research indicates that the danger of an twist of fate rises drastically if the motorist is texting in the back of the wheel. Being in an twist of fate while performing corporate organisation might mirror negatively to your judgment further to on your business enterprise.

E-mail

Electronic mail, normally referred to as e mail, may be very regarded to most students and personnel. It may be used like ext or synchronous chat, and it may be furnished to a cellular cellular phone. In commercial organization, e-mail has basically supplanted print tough duplicate letters for outside (outdoor the commercial organization employer) contact, in addition to assuming the location of memoranda for internal (within the enterprise) conversation. E-mail may be quite useful for communications that have in particular greater substance than a textual content message, even though it remains tremendous implemented for short quick messages.

Many organizations use automated emails to understand remarks from the overall public or to remind colleagues that periodic reviews or payments are due. You also may be assigned to "populate" a form e-mail in which desired paragraphs are utilized however you pick out from a menu of phrases to make the language in shape for a selected transaction.

E-mails can be casual in non-public situations, however enterprise company conversation entails hobby to element, the data that your e mail represents you and your organisation, and a pro tone just so it is able to be transmitted to any 0.33 birthday party if required. E-mails are typically used to speak data interior corporations. Although electronic mail can also have an easygoing vibe, maintain in thoughts that once used for corporation, it has to reflect professionalism and respect. Never write or transmit something which you wouldn't want to be study in public inside the the front of your company president.

Tips for Effective Business Emails

Proper salutations have to carry recognize and save you mixture-united states of america of americain case a communique is through danger introduced to the incorrect character. For example, use a greeting like "Dear Ms. X" (outside) or "Hi Jerry" (inner) (internal).

Subject traces need to be precise, succinct, and unique. This lets in the receiver realize the substance of the message. For instance, "Proposal associated" or "Your query of 10/25."

Close with a signature. Identify your self via way of installing a signature block that automatically consists of your call and business enterprise touch facts.

Avoid abbreviations. An electronic mail is not a text message, and the readers won't find out your humor cause to roll on the floor laughing out loud.

Be short. Omit vain terms.

Use a proper layout. Include line breaks amongst terms or cut up your content fabric into small paragraphs for ease of studying. A terrific email ought to get to the thing and bring about 3 concise paragraphs or fewer.

Reread, rewrite, and assessment. Catch and restore spelling and grammatical problems earlier than you hit "ship." It will take greater time and effort to remedy the harm produced with the resource of manner of a moved speedy, badly worded email than to do it efficiently the primary time.

Reply proper now. Watch out for an emotional response—in no manner react in anger—however create a workout of answering all emails inside twenty-4 hours, even if truely to united states of america that you could deliver the desired facts in 40-eight or seventy- hours.

Use "Reply All" cautiously. Do now not ship your reply to everybody who had been given the primary e mail until your message defini be visible thru the whole organization.

Caps are used at the Internet to talk empathic emotion or yelling and are taken into consideration impolite.

Test hyperlinks. If you add a hyperlink, take a look at it to ensure it's far complete.

E-mail earlier of time in case you are going to attach big files (audio and seen files are typically rather huge) to keep away from exceeding the recipient's mailbox restriction or activating the unsolicited mail clear out.

Give remarks or study up. If you don't get preserve of a reaction in twenty-4 hours, e mail or smartphone. Spam filters can also furthermore have intercepted your message, consequently your recipient can also moreover in no manner have received it.

Chapter 24: Netiquette Takeaways

Many people are energetic in our online interactions and understand its rewards: finding out new information fast, setting up new pals and connections, and maybe feeling like we aren't on my own in our sports and ideals.

But all of this get right of access to and impact comes with its norms and hints of behavior. After all, we don't need to alienate ourselves or get into social or prison difficulty.

It's vital to have a look at the netiquette norms and, occasionally, remind ourselves that regardless of the truth that we also can see unfeeling characters on our displays, there are real humans inside the lower back of the ones terms who will experience real feelings after they look at what we positioned up online.